HERNE BAY
IN OLD PHOTOGRAPHS

THESE BOATMEN have been photographed by Pemberton on the beach below the bottom of Richmond Street. It is interesting to note the height of the shingle relative to the promenade and Tower Gardens in this early photograph (see also p. 39 top). The curious catch proudly displayed between them is a large clump of Goose Barnacles (*Lepas anatifera*). These normally live in the open sea where they attach themselves to floating objects, and are often cast ashore after storms. It is difficult to see if this clump is actually attached to a piece of wreckage or not.

HERNE BAY
IN OLD PHOTOGRAPHS

COLLECTED BY
JOHN HAWKINS

ALAN SUTTON

Alan Sutton Publishing Limited
Phoenix Mill · Far Thrupp · Stroud · Gloucestershire

First published 1991

British Library Cataloguing in Publication Data

Herne Bay in old photographs.
I. Hawkins, John, 1951–
942.234

ISBN 0-86299-891-3

Typeset in 9/10 Korinna.
Typesetting and origination by
Alan Sutton Publishing Limited.
Printed in Great Britain by
The Bath Press, Avon.

CONTENTS

HERNE BAY FIRE BRIGADE. This fine portrait was produced at Shepherds Corner Studios. The number 7 on the uniform indicates that this man was among the earliest group of volunteers along with such well known names as Wacher, White, Adams, Ingleton and Welby. The arm badge indicates he was also an ambulance man; it is the badge of The British Red Cross Society National Fire Brigade Union (see p. 22).

INTRODUCTION

This selection of photographs is drawn from my own collection which has been put together over the last twenty years. The format chosen does not attempt to reflect the history of the town in chronological order; the selection of material used is essentially personal. Where gaps occur in coverage, this may indicate a shortage of suitable material or just the limitations of time and space.

The town of Herne Bay has experienced two distinct periods of growth separated by something of a depression. The first burst of activity was around 1800, the second was towards the end of the nineteenth century. In the 1790s people were beginning to consider the various benefits of sea bathing. An obvious place for the new bathing machines was the beach to the east of the Ship Inn. The Ship had been established here for many years catering for the trade generated by the coastal trading vessels, or Hoys, that used this part of the bay for collecting and landing their cargoes. Local trade must have been improved with visitors to the sea side arriving on the old road from Canterbury. In turn the establishment of a military encampment on the East Cliff also attracted visitors and provided more local business. By the 1820s a small grid of streets was laid out off the road that ran back from the sea front inland to Herne and on to Canterbury. This modest beginning was perhaps the first of the speculative developments by a land owner hoping to take advantage of the attractions of the seaside.

The London-based developers of the 1830s employed considerable artistic licence when preparing the engraved illustrations for their capital-raising prospectuses. A tradition of optimistically illustrating a concept rather than the reality has continued through a variety of grandiose local schemes right up to the 1990s.

For contemporary images of this first phase of growth we must rely on drawings, prints and paintings.

When considering the second surge of growth towards the end of the nineteenth century it is interesting to compare the following quotes. In a town guide of 1891 the introduction reads ' . . . a town that must shortly be well planned, well patronised, and well out of its mysterious stagnation.' The equivalent passage in a 1927 guide reads 'Few places are so favourably placed as this delightful holiday resort. Situtated on the north coast of Kent, commanding extensive views of the open sea Herne Bay is indeed an ideal place either for residence or holiday.'

The development of practical photography happily coincides with this second phase of growth. The local photographers Craik, Pemberton, Palmer, Lowe, Scrivens, Simmons and others have, through their work, provided us with a window on to the events, both ordinary and spectactular, that were part of life in the town during its progression from 'stagnation' to 'delight'.

This selection includes pictures from the late 1860s through to the 1940s. Most of the material used dates from the early 1900s, the 'golden years' of the Edwardian seaside resort. Photographs of the town before the 1880s are not common; most that are known have been published previously and are therefore not included in this book.

Local history is essentially about people; Herne Bay has had its share of magnificent staged events and these are illustrated. Also included are scenes that somehow caught the photographer's eye but then perhaps got no further than a family album. All have some part to play in telling the story of the town's development.

This collection is by no means unique, and with luck this publication may stimulate interest in similar material and more people will come forward to put names to mystery faces. I hope that readers will gain as much pleasure from looking at these pictures as I have in collecting them over the years.

SECTION ONE

Disasters

Floods – Storms – Pier Strikes – Landslips – Wrecks
Frozen Seas – Fires

MARKET STREET UNDERWATER. This scene was photographed on Monday 29 November 1897 and has been repeated many times since. On this occasion strong winds from the North West drove the seas over the length of the front from Roger's Marine Baths (below the East Cliff) to St George's Baths in the west (below St George's Terrace). By the time of high tide boats were being used to rescue women and children from Market Street, Beach Street, along Sunnyside and Richmond Street. The area bounded by Mortimer Street to the north, Beach Street to the east and High Street to the south was at the time building land, and this was all under water. Promenade Central suffered badly with hundreds of pounds worth of damage to property and stock. Much of the damage was caused by timbers from the old pier and Hampton pier serving as battering rams in the waves. Dr Fenoulhet had the novel experience of being rowed along the seafront to visit a patient. There was no loss of human life in this disaster although many people lost livestock. The ostler of the New Dolphin lost all his fowl, and Mr Collard of the Tower Hotel managed to save nine of his ten horses but his favourite riding pony was drowned trying to escape from the rising water in the stable yard behind the hotel. This picture was one of six used by the *Herne Bay Press* on Saturday 4 December 1897. This was the first occasion on which they used a number of photographs in this way.

THE MOST SEVERE GALES to hit the town since 1897 blew through Saturday and Sunday 10 and 11 March 1906. The wind combined with spring tides meant that by 11.30 on Monday morning the sea was well above the normal high water mark (high tide was not until 1.14 p.m.). This picture shows Market Street once more under water. The experience of 1897 meant that forewarned by two days of gales, many people had plugged their doors with clay to minimize water entry. By all accounts this system was most successful.

THE PHOTOGRAPHER PEMBERTON could almost have taken this picture from the doorway of his shop. The islands in the rising flood water are the spoil from a hole dug by two men from the gas board. They abandoned their work as the water flooded over the roadway, leaving their hand-cart to its watery fate.

THE MAIN DAMAGE to the sea defences occurred at the ramp in front of the Ship Hotel. The sea washed the fill out from behind the timber breastwork, causing the roadway and ramp over to collapse. Several businesses on the seafront had installed metal shutters in anticipation of such a storm. Despite the height of the water, damage was not as costly as the 1897 storm.

THESE FIVE PICTURES were available to the public in the week following the storm and before the *Herne Bay Press* was published on 17 March. At Hampton the seas had washed right through some of the houses, and a cottage at the north end was described as uninhabitable.

TAKEN IN FRONT OF MARINE TERRACE, this photograph shows a light covering of snow that fell on Tuesday. This must have added to the misery of the people trying to dry out their homes.

NOT ALL STORMS ARRIVE IN WINTER MONTHS. On 18 July 1924 a north-west gale combined with a high tide to cause considerable damage particularly on the beach west of the pier. Mr Holness lost forty-two bathing cabins from St George's Baths (see p. 68). At the opposite end of the town all the cabins at the East Cliff bathing station were washed back on to the parade (see p. 56). The Frolics concert party lost their stage at Lane End. This photograph shows some of the smashed timber driven into the corner of the beach just next to the pier. The town was quick to rally round: Mr G. Cursons, the Chairman of the HBUDC, organized a town meeting on the Saturday and £250 was collected within twenty-four hours. Many of the local boatmen either received new boats bought out of this fund, or were able to borrow private boats while theirs were being repaired.

A WRECKED ENGINE SHED marks the path of a whirlwind. The morning of Saturday 17 November 1906 started fine with the wind in the south-west. There was slight drizzle followed by heavier rain, but by 1.30 p.m. dense black clouds had appeared. The darkness was later compared to a similar phenomenon experienced at the time of the Mount Pelee disaster some three years earlier. The storm which lasted only a few minutes left a trail of damage one hundred yards wide stretching from the south-west beyond the railway station to Hillborough in the north-east. This whole three mile trail was littered with debris. At Greenhill the tops were torn off haystacks; in Central Avenue a Mr J.W. Henley had to cling to a post in his garden as he could not get back into his house quickly enough; gardens in Gordon Road and Stanley Road were flattened, including their sheds and fences and the end of the roof and ridge tiles were taken off the school buildings in Kings Road. This engine shed which was on Mickleburgh Hill belonged to Mr H.E. Ramsey. It was completely wrecked with timbers carried by the wind some fifty or sixty yards. In the local newspaper the following week the photographer Pemberton was advertising seven photo-postcards 1s 6d post free entitled 'In the track of the Whirlwind'. This same storm brought some good luck to a man named Young of Hampton Hill. While walking on the beach he found a tusk sticking from the sand, and on digging round he found a second. One was 3ft 4in from tip to tip, the other, almost complete, was 4ft 11in around the curve. These mammoth remains were acquired by Mr E.W. Turner MA of the Herne Bay College where they were placed in the boys' museum. Similar finds can now be seen in the Herne Bay Museum above the library.

THE CLAY AND SAND CLIFFS to the east of the town are not noted for their stability. The most spectacular slips were recorded by local photographers particularly when buildings were threatened (as in 1904). This slip in 1909 shows graphically the result of a rotational slip with the clay pushing the broken groynes up from below. The slip followed a period of heavy snow and severe frosts (the *Herne Bay Press* of 20 March reported that over three feet of snow had fallen since the beginning of the month, an average of two inches per day). So bad was the weather that the Herne point to point races at Chestfield were cancelled. When considering the scale of this slip it is a sobering thought that the workmen pictured face their repair task armed with hand tools.

FLOODED STREETS have never been uncommon in the lowest parts of the town. Even with the improved drainage schemes of the 1990s Kings Road is still liable to flooding if a couple of road gullies get blocked by leaves or debris. In this picture a small boy is seen making the best of things close to the back fence of Philp & Whitteridges timber yard. The hand-cart in the flooded forecourt beyond belongs to the plumbers A. Stewart & Son.

THIS REMARKABLE PICTURE WAS TAKEN BY LOWE in the early hours of Thursday morning 6 August 1908. At about 3.00 a.m. J.S. White of the Divers Arms heard cries for help. As he looked out to sea the barge *Caleb* was settling on the bottom some 100 yd offshore. The skipper, mate and a labourer had climbed up the rigging to the cross trees in order to escape the water. The barge, belonging to a Mr Chapman, was loaded with seventy tons of stone kerbing intended for delivery to Mr Head who was engaged on constructing New Road Grand Drive. Unable to unload on the Wednesday, the barge anchored offshore. The north-west wind veered to the north-east and in the small hours the wind got up and swept away the ship's boat. With the decks awash the rigging was slowly being torn apart, and the mizen mast was swept away tearing a section of deck with it. With no means of getting a line to the barge a call was put in to the Margate lifeboat. Under sail the crew took about an hour to reach Herne Bay. By anchoring outside the barge, the lifeboat was able to swing down towards the trapped men. With the skipper last to go, the men jumped into the water to be pulled out by the lifeboatmen. With some temporary repairs to a damaged rudder the lifeboat ran down to Whitstable. This incident led to two gentlemen, Mr E. Renton and Mr E.J. Duveen, donating a rocket apparatus to the town for just such an emergency. A building was erected to house the apparatus close to the pier entrance (see p. 60 top).

CONSIDERABLE DAMAGE WAS CAUSED to the pier by the impact of the barge *Clara*. The *Clara*, owned by Mr Solly of Whitstable and captained by Mr Edward Benney, had come down to Herne Bay from London on 20 October 1905. The cargo was timber and oats. She arrived in the morning and anchored to the north-east of the pier head but by 11.30 that night she had dragged her anchor and drifted on to the pier. The mate somehow managed to climb up the rigging and scramble on to the pier deck, whereupon he ran to fetch the coastguard. In the best tradition of the sea the captain stayed on board. The coastguard was unable to help and most of the damage was caused between 2.00 and 3.00 a.m. With the assistance of Mr C. Mount the barge was eventually brought off at around 5.00 a.m. (by which time the tide would have turned). Although the photographer has got to the seaward side of the damage, spectators and the pier tram can be seen stopped short at the previous bay.

IT WAS PARTICULARLY COLD during the second week of February 1929 when this photograph was taken; there was never less than eleven degrees of frost. On Tuesday 12 February the temperature at four o'clock in the afternoon had dropped to nineteen degrees fahrenheit. It was reported at the time that the sea had last frozen in 1895. There was ice skating on the dykes at Reculver and Broomfield pond (see p. 138 bottom). The coldest day of the year recorded at Greenwich observatory for 1911 was 15 February at twelve degrees fahrenheit.

THE TOWN HALL was destroyed by fire on 12 June 1925. At about ten o'clock in the morning smoke was seen rising from the north end of the hall. With their premises next door in the High Street, the brigade did not have to travel very far (see p. 84 bottom). This was one fire that the famous Captain Wacher missed as he was out of town. It was perhaps fitting that Lieut. C.W. Welby should be in charge of the brigade on this occasion as his father had built the hall. Both photographs were taken by Scrivens; such money making opportunities did not crop up every day. Scrivens obviously had his skates on as these postcards were for sale in the afternoon; this view looking down the side of the building was posted in the early evening on Friday 12 June.

THIS PICTURE BY PALMER shows the inside of the burnt out hall looking towards the High Street. The steel frame of the rear balcony can be seen as well as the metal frames of seating on the floor. The fire spread over the fire station and through the council offices to the left in this picture. As officials tried to rescue papers and ledgers there were cries from the crowd to 'let the — rate books burn'.

THE PIER THEATRE WAS DESTROYED BY FIRE on the night of Sunday 9 September 1928. The fire was discovered at eleven o'clock and the alarm was raised by Cecil Baker using the new telephone kiosk by the old rocket house (see p. 59 bottom). The glow from the fire could be seen for thirty miles and people drove from as far away as Faversham and Margate to watch the blaze which was brought under control by three o'clock in the morning. This photograph by Lowe & Co must have been produced in some haste. The negative has been reversed in printing so what you see here is a handed version of the real scene (the correct view can be seen by looking at the photograph in a mirror).

ON MONDAY MORNING crowds gathered to stare at the remains of the building where so many of them had spent happy hours. With hindsight it is interesting to read the local newspapers from the spring of 1884; each week there was more news about the new pavilion (as the Pier Theatre was originally known). The editorial comment in the *Herne Bay Press* of 24 May 1884 is particularly relevant. 'We would impress upon the authorities the importance of having all the spaces under the floor of the pavilion well cleared from shavings or other inflammable materials or a stray half extinguished fusee [match], may one day convest the whole into ruins.'

THE RUINS WERE STILL SMOKING early Monday morning. The business to the right of the picture was a café. One witness of the fire has told me how he helped the owner rescue stock and equipment from the premises as the fire spread sideways from the central part of the theatre. When the heat and smoke made further salvage trips impossible they came out on to the pavement only to find that the bulk of the plated items that they had rescued had disappeared into the dark crowd of spectators.

THE FIREMEN tidying up on Monday morning are, left to right: Frank Hobbs, Charlie Cossey, Norman Ells (with the axe), -?-, Foreman Harris, -?-, -?-, ? Hutchins, Dick Wild.

SEPTEMBER 1928 was a spectacular month for fires at Herne Bay. This the 'Casino' fire was number three. The fire was spotted by two boatmen Gilbert Heathcote and A. Pressley as they were returning from a fishing trip just after midnight. They raised the brigade and alerted neighbours to the danger. With the help of the Whitstable brigade the fire took four hours to control. The ballroom and restaurant with the four shops below were all a total loss. It was reported that Ralph Fiddlers orchestra who were appearing at the Casino lost their instruments, music and a bicycle. The site was redeveloped with a new cinema and single storey restaurant.

HOPEFULLY, PUBLISHING THIS PICTURE will enable more names to be put to faces. The event could be any one of a number where the brigade and local 'big-wigs' were assembled in front of the pier theatre. Perhaps it is an Empire Day gathering. Working left to right from the top down: -?-, -?-, -?-; second row: -?-, -?-, Jimmy White (see p. 85 top), -?-, Fred Wacher, Captain Welby, -?-; third row: -?-, -?-, -?-; standing on the ground: -?-, -?-, ? Hall, -?-, -?-, -?-, -?-, H.E. Ramsey, -?-, -?-, -?-, -?-, ? Mackey, -?-, Foreman Norman Ells, ? Rowden, -?-; on the ground: Josh Hammond, -?-, -?-, -?-, -?-, ? Shelley, -?-.

SECTION TWO

Transport

Planes – Paddle Steamers – Brakes – Motor Wagonettes
Steam Buses – Delivery Vehicles

M. Salmet coming to earth

MORE PEOPLE THAN USUAL were anxiously studying the weather on 13 August 1912. This was the day scheduled for a plane to actually land at Herne Bay. Under the enterprise of the *Daily Mail* Monsieur Henri Salmet was touring the country and giving flying demonstrations around the coast. In preparation a field belonging to Mr C.J. Sinden at Underdown Farm, Eddington had been marked with a large white cross. A good crowd had been gathering at the field since the early afternoon. The *Daily Mail* were represented at the field by Mr Stokes and Mr Thomas, their cars being prominently labelled 'Daily Mail Aeroplane Circuit'. At 4.45 p.m. a dark speck was seen to the north west – the Bleriot monoplane was following the coast at some 800 ft. The pilot turned south over Beltinge and turned again at Herne windmill, he descended, cut figures of eight, switch-backed and volplaned. He swooped low over the field and rose to disappear in the clouds. Salmet eventually descended in a graceful curve and landed gently. As the crowd moved forward a barrier of poles was created by the boy scouts of the 9th Battersea (St Mark's). This must have been an unparalleled bonus to their holiday camp under Scoutmaster Grieg. The crowd cheered first Salmet and then the *Daily Mail*. In a short speech the pilot joked that there was plenty of room in the sky, with no speed restrictions. Some of the spectators should learn to fly so that on another visit they could have a race. Salmet left the field to more cheering and took tea with Mr Sinden. On his return he checked over the machine and 'oiled up'. Under threatening skies he took off, turning to wave to the crowd before following the railway line towards Margate and his next scheduled landing at Broadstairs. He had left Gravesend at 4.15 p.m. and covered the 35 mile journey in some 30 minutes.

M. Salmet visits Herne Bay.

1096. *S.E.C Aviation Town. 1921.*
Manager Sydney F. Woods.
Communications G.P.O. Herne Bay.

A DE HAVILLAND DUNG HUNTER, this jazzy looking plane is a DH6 designed by De Havilland and built by Airco. The plane originated in 1916 as a two-seater trainer to meet the demands of the rapidly expanding Royal Flying Corps. As with most contemporary types of aircraft the greater part of its structure was built from spruce. Following the entry of the United States of America into the war in 1917 the supply of this timber virtually ceased and full production did not really get going until late 1917/early 1918. This particular example had the military serial number B2861 and like many others it was sold off in 1919. The very docile nature of the plane made it ideal for the popular pleasure flights that were being run by enterprising young pilots almost anywhere a flat field could be found near a town or seaside resort. In 1921 Sydney Woods almost certainly had this photograph taken for publicity purposes. The name below the kangaroo motif is IKANOPIT and the Australian nickname for this aircraft was Dung Hunter. G-EANJ was withdrawn from the civil register in April 1922.

THE *AUDREY* WAS RUNNING ON THE ROUTE from Rochester to Herne Bay, calling at Southend and Sheerness in 1923; this route was also worked by the *Princess of Wales*. In May 1923 trade was so good that both boats were used and the local paper reports that over 700 people were landed at Herne Bay. A trip from Chatham to Herne Bay cost 2s (10p) with a return at 3s 9d (about 19p), the return journey being by rail. In addition to the coastal route the *Audrey* also ran daily trips out to the Girdler light (today replaced by a steel beacon). This hour long excursion cost adults 1s 6d (7½p) and children 1s. This photograph shows a band assembled by the side of the funnel on what may be just such a trip.

THE PADDLE STEAMER *AUDREY* was one of the smaller paddle steamers to call at Herne Bay. Captain S.J. Shippick had operated her on the south coast in 1914. In the early years of the war he worked her on charter to the Admiralty, taking men to the Kingsnorth airship works. In 1915 Audrey was bought by the Admiralty to continue similar ferry duties but in 1922 Captain Shippick re-purchased *Audrey* on behalf of the New Medway Steam Packet Company. Captain Shippick went on to become the company's Managing Director. Working with Captain T.J. Aldis they opened up various new routes and it was Captain Aldis who first took command of *Audrey* on the regular service to Herne Bay.

THE *MEDWAY QUEEN* IS PERHAPS THE BEST REMEMBERED PADDLE STEAMER that called at Herne Bay. She was built by the Ailsa Shipbuilding and Engineering Co. Ltd at Toon in 1924. She had the advantage of a promenade deck from bow to stern, her gross tonnage was 316 and she was almost 180 ft long. Her arrival with the New Medway Steam Packet Company meant that the smaller *Audrey* could be released to run other services from Herne Bay to Margate and Ramsgate. As a small child playing on the beach and cliffs at Hampton I can remember that tea-time coincided with the *Medway Queen* berthing at the pierhead. The plume of black smoke above the horizon provided the warning signal to get back to the beach hut. In addition to providing pleasure to thousands of trippers the *Medway Queen* saw duty with the Admiralty through the 1939–45 conflict. At the Dunkirk evacuation this little ship completed seven trips across the channel saving over 7,000 men. On her last trip, although she was badly damaged and posted missing, she somehow managed to limp home. After being released from Admiralty service she was completely refitted at Southampton. From 1947 she once again gave pleasure to millions of trippers on various routes. 1963 saw her last full season running from Herne Bay to Southend. By 1965 the fare had risen to 10s (50p) return, with children half price; combined rail and steamer tickets were also available. Her survival in recent years has depended almost totally on thousands of hours of work put in by volunteer conservationists. Their work may yet save a small but significant piece of our marine heritage.

THE TOWER HOTEL AND RESTAURANT in the Parade had been built up as a business through the late 1800s by J.W. Collard. This picture showing a couple of brakes full of customers eager for a day out was taken around 1900, soon after the business had passed to J. Dyke. Dyke advertised that excursions could be arranged with charabancs or brakes for any number. There were livery stables to the rear with saddle-horses, landaus, victorias and dog carts for hire.

THE GOVERNESS CART was the state of the art as far as personal horse-drawn transport was concerned in the early 1900s. The name derives from the idea that the vehicle was thought suitable for children. The cart was difficult to fall out of and the door was some distance from the dangerous parts of the horse. The walk from the pony's head to the door at the back meant that ponies were sometimes known to start off before the driver was in place. The lady with the parasol is sitting in the normal driving position. This example has the usual full elliptic springs; the mudguards and lamps were something of a refinement. The small child with the teddy is believed to be the young Miss Lane. She is perhaps best remembered by many in the town organising her staff in the Mortimer Street shop next to the Congregational church (see p. 82).

THE VEHICLE IN THE FOREGROUND OF THIS PICTURE parked opposite the Royal Hotel (now the Bun Penny) can lay claim to two notable firsts. D1061 was the first motor vehicle to join the horse brakes working from the seafront; it was also the first motor vehicle used to run a service to Canterbury from a base in Herne Bay. D1061 was an 18 cwt 6 h.p. Daimler wagonette and was registered as a public conveyance on the 24 March 1904 by A.L. Strong, a local bailiff and debt collector of Tottenham. The *Herne Bay Press* of May 1904 carried an advert for weekday trips to Reculver and Grove Ferry as well as a Sunday morning service to Canterbury. The business was run by Thomas Taylor-Strong (A.L. was his father). In 1905 Taylor-Strong purchased other vehicles and was involved with the South East and Chatham Railway. However, the venture running between Herne Bay station and Canterbury West was not a success. The resumed limited service between the town and the city departed from opposite the Royal Hotel at 10.45 a.m., returning from the Saracens Head at Canterbury at 12.45 p.m. The single fare was 1s 6d (7½p), 2s return (10p). As in 1904 the afternoons were used for running tours.

THE VEHICLE PICTURED HERE in front of Hillborough church is a Daimler Wagonette registered A3888. The lettering on the vehicle's side (below the driver) is the only known evidence of any connection with the East Kent & Herne Bay Motor Omnibus Co. Ltd. The driver would appear to be a Mr J.E. West who ran his own service between Herne Bay and Canterbury in 1909. In 1910, West may also have run A3888 between Whitstable and Herne Bay.

THIS FINE SINGLE DECK STEAM BUS had been ordered from Messrs Thomas Clarkson of Chelmsford for delivery by 25 March 1906 ready to commence service at Easter. (The registration F1806 was made in Essex on 7 April 1906.) The East Kent and Herne Bay Motor Omnibus Co. Ltd had also ordered a double-decker from the same company but this did not arrive until May. In March the *Herne Bay Press* carried adverts for four journeys each way between Canterbury and Herne Bay. In its first seven days of work F1806 carried upward of 600 passengers. The twenty seats were found to be insufficient and many people had to be turned away. Archibald Glover Iggulden was a principal of this venture along with Herbert E. Ramsey and Nathaniel Rowden, all names that in their time were to be associated with the growth and development of the town. In the photograph Iggulden can be seen standing at the front of the vehicle (next to the man in uniform who is probably a postman from Philpott's premises next door).

THIS COMMER VEHICLE, registration D9578, was purchased by F.W. Wacher in April 1913; it was the third motor passenger vehicle to join their fleet. It was finally disposed of in September 1920 having done sterling service on local routes both under the Wacher banner and from 1916 as part of the East Kent Road Car Company. This picture was taken on the west side of Dolphin Street almost opposite Wacher's stables, yard and offices. The man on the left is a driver thought to be Mr Jim Crouch. Although well established with a number of businesses locally, Frederick Wacher had not been involved with the earliest development of motorised public transport in the town. However in 1912 he succeeded J.E. West with the service between Herne Bay and Canterbury. Wacher was able to use his considerable business acumen and experience in haulage (both steam and horse powered) to good advantage in this new venture. His success was such that F.W. Wacher & Co. Ltd was the only fully independent company to become a constituent of East Kent in 1916. Known as Captain Wacher through his connection with the fire service (see p. 22), F.W. was a respected figure and held a place on the East Kent board until his death in 1933.

W. HADFIELD BAKER first appears in local trade directories in 1903. His shop premises with bakery behind were on the south-west corner of Charles Street and East Street. The previous baker, George Hooper, had been there since 1893 with A. Wilkinson before him since 1886. Hadfield traded until 1927 when another local baker William Swain took the premises. The name Hadfield remained etched in the frosted glass shop door until the building was demolished in the 1970s. The horse-drawn delivery van with its fine example of the sign writer's art was photographed outside Mason Terrace in what was then Kings Road East (opposite the Council Schools). In 1903 Herne Bay's population of 10,393 was served by thirteen bakers. The 1988 population of 31,750 would require thirty-nine bakers to maintain the same ratio. Excluding the supermarkets the local directories list only seven.

SHEPHERD NEAME LIMITED had stores and agents spread throughout Kent. Deliveries were sent out from the brewery at Faversham by rail, traction engine and latterly motor lorry. This is typical of those vehicles used for local deliveries in Station Road and was based at the store behind the Railway Commercial Hotel (now the Four Fathoms). The man with the white beard is the licensee J. Goodall, and the horse was named Dolly.

HERNE BAY RAILWAY STATION SEEN FROM COBBLERS BRIDGE. The railway had come to Herne Bay in 1861, the original station being west of Greenhill Bridge. The main station building we see today (and in this picture) was opened in 1863. In the distance the hills to the east of the town are virtually free of buildings. The area to the south is open parkland with isolated mature trees.

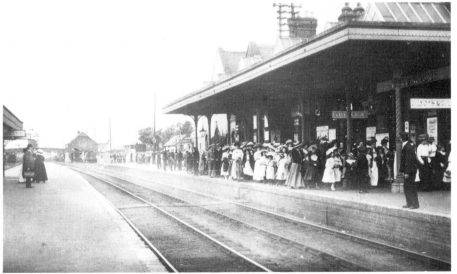

VISITORS CROWD THE PLATFORM in this picture of Herne Bay railway station. I am sure that passengers then were happier to put up with a little jostling on the platform than are many of today's passengers (and drivers) sitting in a queue on the M2. In August 1909 when the Royal Engineers came to the town (see p. 97 top) the excuse given for there being no formal welcome was that the rail network was so busy that their arrival time could not be guaranteed.

JIM CROUCH seems to have been a driver for at least two local companies. This photograph shows him in the uniform of the laundry in Kings Road. The hat and jacket do not seem to be of the same vintage. The hat band proudly states Herne Bay Steam Laundry, although after about 1907 or 1908 the business changed its title to become the Herne Bay and Canterbury Laundry, as the lettering on the collars. Perhaps the hat was a comfortable old favourite. Jim can also be seen alongside Wacher's bus in Richmond Street (see p. 31).

THIS VIEW OF THE CLOCK TOWER was taken some time before 1910. The man with the horse and cart that appears to be in the middle of the road is in all probability turning to the right to call at the premises of Herbert Henry Boulding, wine and spirit merchant of 9 Promenade Central (now the headquarters of the Herne Bay Angling Association). The strange vehicle travelling in the opposite direction is a small two-wheeled trap of some sort being pulled by a man on a bicycle.

Seafront

Tower Gardens – Promenade Central – The East Cliff – The Pier
The Bandstand – St George's Baths - The West Cliff

ONE OF THE EARLIEST PICTURES USED IN THIS BOOK is this picture of the seafront in the 1870s. The mill in the centre was pulled down in 1878 to be replaced by Sea View Square (see p. 87 top) and Parade Villas. The large building to the right of the mill (now Richmond House on the corner of Richmond Street) was originally built as a hotel, The Kent. In turn this building has been a private house, a girls' school and a YMCA hostel (see p. 88 top). The lower building between the two started out in life as Herne Bay's first railway terminal to the west of Greenhill Bridge. When the line was extended through to Thanet the building was removed and rebuilt on the front as a public house. The seafront itelf is virtually undeveloped, although a token number of groynes appear to arrest the longshore drift of shingle along the coast. Retention of beach material in front of the town exercises the minds of those in authority and strains the pockets of residents to this day.

EARLY SEASIDE ENTERTAINERS are notoriously hard to find in photographs. This part of the beach below the Clock Tower is known to have been used by the Herne Bay Minstrels in the 1890s. The troupe seen here are entertaining a small group of children and adults. They are using the absolute minimum of props, such alfresco performances obviously depending heavily on favourable weather. In the background is the short second pier which was opened in 1873, while beyond the pier are the bathing machines of St George's Baths. A barge can be seen unloading on the open beach. The large white building is the Coast Guard Station standing below what is now Albany Drive. Almost the whole of the West Cliff is undeveloped. In the far distance the old Hampton Oyster Company pier can be seen, abandoned and collapsing but with at least half of its solid infill still in place.

THE SECOND AND SHORTEST PIER AT HERNE BAY was opened by the Lord Mayor of London in August 1873. Unlike the first deep sea pier which had been demolished in 1871, this second pier was only 320 ft long and could not provide a landing point for steamers. Originally it had a small bandstand at the seaward end but in 1884 a theatre and shops were added at the entrance. This photograph was taken by J. Craik who traded in Canterbury and Herne Bay. One of his shops can be seen on the near right, at the eastern end of the row of shops.

THIS VIEW OF TOWER GARDENS LOOKING EAST was probably taken from the roof of the Pier Theatre in about 1900. The formal gardens were much as they were when laid out to celebrate Queen Victoria's Jubilee in 1887. The shelter in the foreground is one of two that were paid for by public subscription although the original plans show four. The flagstaff in the centre was the gift of a Mr F.W. Fairbrass of Telford House. Looking along the promenade the change in colour shows where it had recently been extended. On the beach between the first and second breakwaters there is an upright piano on a makeshift platform. This was most certainly not an approved site for alfresco entertainment and no doubt the town beadle, Mr Adolphus Boorman, would be doing his best to make sure that the nuisance was removed.

THE TOWER GARDENS WERE ENCLOSED BY A FENCE which consisted of stout oak posts about 3ft 9in high connected by three iron railings. This fence was obviously a good strong job as it protected properties along the front from floating baulks of timber in the great storms in 1897 and 1906. Some lengths of it could still be seen in place in the 1930s. This family group with their delicate iron-wheeled cane-bodied baby carriage seem to be preparing to go on to the beach. The iron gate through the fence was one of ten giving access to the gardens with their gravel paths, lawns and flower beds. The black Italian poplars and shrubs that formed part of the original scheme had virtually disappeared by 1890.

THE PLAN OF THE TOWER GREEN IMPROVEMENTS was published in March 1887. This view is looking west from below Richmond Street. The grassed areas to either side of the Clock Tower had long been a local joke: these 'greens' were known as the 'browns'. New formal gardens were seen as an appropriate civic gesture to celebrate Victoria's Jubilee. Subscription lists were opened and committees set up to organize fund raising events. The works were laid out by the council engineer Mr G. Wallace and surveyor Mr Alan Collard, while the labour was provided by Mr Cade of the nursery in Avenue Road. The gardens were in part made up by using surplus soil from the new schools site in Kings Road. Despite the efforts of gardeners few trees of shrubs survive the exposed nature of the site for long and the beds were planted out each year.

THIS VIEW OF THE EAST END OF TOWER GARDENS shows one of the elements of the 1887 scheme that has survived past its hundredth birthday. In January 1887 Henry C. James (of the Pier Company) appealed for funds to build shelters proposed for each end of the gardens. The appeal was successful and by May, Boulton & Paul had supplied two Arboretum Shelters (Ref No. 339) from their Rose Lane Works at Norwich. Constructed from red deal with Canadian pattern iron roofs, these seemed to have been a pretty good buy at £60 each. in 1895 Boulton & Paul illustrated the shelters in their catalogue as 'Jubilee Memorial as erected by us at Herne Bay'.

JOHN 'NIMBLE' QUICK was a well-known character in the town around the turn of the century. Quick amused visitors and locals alike with his tales of how the town had been years before. He was also reckoned to be a fair judge at forecasting the weather. Quick lived at No. 30 King Street (between Beach Street and William Street, now part of Kings Road). In August 1908 the owner applied for an Ejection Order at St Augustine's Petty Sessions. The chairman of the bench was F.H. Wilbee, and despite establishing that Quick was both very ill and very old, he was given twenty-one days to quit on the basis that the house was in a filthy state and unfit for habitation. Quick died in January 1911.

THE NEW CONNAUGHT HOTEL replaced the old wooden building known as 'The Hall by the Sea' (see p. 36). The Connaught was opened in the 1890s by Mr G.H. Boncey who had previously run the Portland Hotel at Greenwich. This hotel with its 'smoking saloons' was much used by local clubs and institutions. For many years it served as the headquarters for the Herne Bay Angling Association.

THIS LINE OF HORSE-DRAWN BRAKES on the seafront was photographed in 1910. In the background it is just possible to make out the crane arm which was in use on the pier for the construction of the new pavilion. Each driver appears to be wearing his official badge as described in section 18 of the Herne Bay Urban District Council bye-laws. By this time motor vehicles were rapidly becoming a recognized means of public transport rather than a novelty. Some of the drivers who spent their winter months hauling goods delivered by barges and who relied on this seasonal holiday trade were perhaps beginning to consider the impact that motor vehicles might have on their incomes.

THE BEACH BELOW WILLIAM STREET around 1905. This picture clearly shows the relative levels of shingle and road which were of most interest to the owners of the properties opposite, particularly when considering the view seen in the picture at the bottom of p. 11. In the foreground lines can be seen securing a barge being unloaded up the slipway roughly where the cameraman is standing. The yacht in the distance below the ship is almost certainly the *Duchess of York* (see p. 49). The nearest vessel may be the *Favourite* skippered by Mr Emery although in 1904 she is thought to have had a white painted hull.

PROMENADE CENTRAL SEEN HERE FROM THE SEA around 1904. I am ninety per cent sure that this photograph was taken from a boat. This would be an easy job today with a pocket 35mm camera but not so easy with a bulky plate camera and tripod. This section of beach was often busy with barge traffic and there are some workmen on the water's edge. At the foot of William Street there is a horse-drawn bus with open seating on the top deck and exposed rear stair. Promenade Central was originally developed as a row of shops on what had been vegetable gardens between the terrace of houses just out of the picture to the right and the single-storey building on the left at the bottom of William Street. This was the post office run by A.W.G. Philpott.

ON A BRIGHT SUNNY DAY early in the 1900s this was one of the busiest parts of the seafront. The stall in the foreground standing on the granite setts of the slipway is probably run by one of the Baga family. Through the late 1800s large numbers of itinerant traders moved into resorts such as Herne Bay to take advantage of the crowds of visitors. The difficulties

experienced in controlling such goings on were regularly reported back to the authorities by the beadle. The Jubilee or Tower Fountain looks considerably sharper in this photograph than it does today after more than a hundred years of exposure to the wind and sea.

PROMENADE CENTRAL after the second stage of its development. The picture by Lowe and Co. shows their own premises in the centre to where they had moved from further along the road. Archibald Glover Iggulden was not a man to let the grass grow under his feet. In March 1918 he applied for a licence for music, singing and dancing in respect of Nos 2 and 3 Promenade Central. The plans for conversion for use for cinematograph entertainment were prepared by the local architect R. Messenger ARIBA. As well as the announcement of the Armistice celebrations in November, the *Herne Bay Press* also carried adverts for Iggulden's clearance sale of stock from 'the new cinema' site.

Tower Shelter, Herne Bay.

HERNE BAY CASINO. By 1925 the Casino complex included the new Herne Bay Casino Winter Garden and Ballroom. The ballroom overlooked the front on the first floor and was 90 ft by 60 ft. This venue with its sprung dance floor and the latest Parisian rainbow cornice lighting was extremely popular. Unfortunately it was only to last a few years (see p. 21 bottom). Reserved seats at an evening concert cost 2s 4d (12p). A dinner and dance ticket for the weekend ball which was evening dress only cost 7s 6d (37½p).

Opposite:

THE TOWER GARDEN SHELTER was illustrated in the official town guide for 1923/24 and described along with the West Cliff Shelter as 'still more improvements'. Designed in reinforced concrete with steel and plate glass screens, it had seating for sixty persons and standing room for a further two hundred. A ladies' retiring room was incorporated at the rear. This picture also shows the Jubilee fountain presented to the town in 1888 by Major Davies. The site of the shelter had previously been used for the winter storage of beach boats. In the summer the grassed area was used by entertainers; this was not one of the recognized official pitches but the authorities seem to have turned a blind eye to what was going on. Despite local protest, which was for some reason backed by Spike Milligan, this shelter was demolished in the 1970s. A handsome spread of black tarmac has for some years shown just what the local authority can achieve when given a free hand at landscaping.

THE BEACH BELOW THE SHIP RAMP. A few years after this photograph was taken the ramp and sea defences were badly damaged in the severe storm of 1906 (see pp. 12 & 13). This was where the Gipsons ran their yacht *Duchess of York* (successor to the *Hilda*). The family also ran the 'original sea baths' seen in the background with the angular bay window. A sign painted on the front wall claims that they were prepared to 'send sea water'. The beach is cluttered with equipment: a shrimp push net can be seen as well as snatch-nets that were used to catch the main ingredient for lobster teas. The line of washing marks the limit of their bathing machines; these clothes may well be the bathing suits that had to be worn by patrons for 'preventing any indecent exposure of the persons of the bathers'. It is easy to see why this part of the beach was known as Gipsons Corner.

THE *DUCHESS OF YORK* ran pleasure trips from below the Ship Inn. She had been built at Whitstable in 1897 and was licensed to carry 120 passengers. In March 1901 she was driven ashore in a gale and suffered £200-worth of damage. Such was her popularity that a local fund was raised and she was repaired, and she ended her days as a watch-boat for the oyster company at Whitstable. Her replacement was a motor boat *Albatross*. The *Duchess* was run by two of the four Gipson brothers, Fred seen here on the left and William in the centre. The four boys and their sister were raised by their mother following a tragic accident in 1887. Their father (also Frederick), their brother Jesse and an uncle Mr Smith were drowned off Bishopstone when their small boat capsized. The widow Annie was obviously a capable lady, and after the disaster she was helped by a local fund. In later years she went on to successfully defend her bathing rights against first the local board and then the council. Perhaps the most famous of the brothers were Bert and his younger brother Cecil. In their day they won practically every coast rowing championship that was open to them. The family connection with amateur rowing was maintained through their nephews, the Conrath brothers, who were equally successful oarsmen in later years.

THE SHIP INN OR HOTEL sits in an ideal position to have witnessed the growth of Herne Bay. The earliest coastal trading vessels used the beach in front of The Ship as their landing place. East Street on the right of this picture was the end of the road that linked Canterbury with the sea via Herne. It was on the side of this road that Sir Henry Oxenden first laid out building plots that were to be the starting point for the development of the Old Town. The timber weather-boarded building seen here to the side of The Ship was built to exploit the potential custom of the large numbers of troops moving through the area in the early 1800s, as well as the increased number of visitors being attracted to the seaside.

THIS PRETTY DOUBLE FRONTED COTTAGE in East Cliff Parade is a good example of seaside architecture with all the decorative twiddly bits that make it both attractive and difficult to maintain. The handsome iron uprights and barley sugar rails on the garden wall probably went for salvage in the Second World War. The flag-pole which was looked after by local boatmen has also long since disappeared. This gentlemen's residence was for many years the home of Edwin Dottridge JP (perhaps the figure by the front door). The far end of the terrace was the bath house of Frederick Holness. This was the site of a sea-bathing business as early as the 1790s.

View from the Downs, Herne Bay. 34.

THIS PEACEFUL SCENE includes most of the ingredients of the Edwardian seaside. The yacht *Duchess of York* drifts past on a glassy sea and modest bathers enter the water using the bathing machines of Frederick Holness. This is the most easterly of Herne Bay's three bathing stations. Mr Holness lived in East Cliff Cottage next door to his Bath House, the last building in East Cliff Parade and his machines can be seen spread along the beach towards what is now the King's Hall. All three stations were for the use of men and women although the local bye-laws use thirty-four paragraphs in eleven pages to explain exactly what was and was not allowed. Dress for both sexes was to be from neck to knee; for ladies this must include knickerbocker drawers, as the aim was to 'prevent indecent exposure of the persons'. Sixpence ($2\frac{1}{2}$p) bought the use of a machine for half an hour, a further sixpence was necessary if the bather required the services of an attendant.

Downs Beach, Herne Bay 31.

BATHING MACHINES HAVE TO MAINTAIN THEIR POSITION relative to the water level if they are to ensure the modest entry and exit to and from the sea for which they were designed. At Herne Bay this raising and lowering was carried out using winches or capstans rather than the horses or donkeys that were seen at resorts with gently sloping sandy beaches. Local machines do not seem to have carried advertising slogans for national companies as was seen elsewhere although some were lettered with the name of proprietors. Nos 20, 21, 22 and 23 seem to be an improved pattern with a cantilevered seat down each side allowing double the capacity on the same chassis width. This pattern does not receive any special treatment in the bye-laws which actually have remarkably little to say about the constructions of the machines themselves. The poles sticking up through the water may be to warn boatmen of the hazard of groyne posts. Alternatively they may relate to the bye-laws which limited how close boats were allowed to approach when bathing machines were in use.

THIS EARLY VIEW OF THE DOWNS and the East Cliff Bandstand shows the area prior to the construction of the East Cliff Pavilion in 1903/4. The troupe performing in the foreground may well be the Herne Bay Minstrels although their usual pitch was the beach in front of the Clock Tower (see p. 37). There was considerable competition for the various pitches; in 1902 the council received applications from nine separate groups of entertainers. The small bandstand in the centre of the picture was removed to the council yard in 1902 and by early 1903 it had been re-erected on the West Cliff. It can still be seen below Bognor Drive, its appearance somewhat compromised by neglect and unsympathetic alterations over the last half century.

THE AREA SEEN IN THIS VIEW looking west over the Downs (in about 1910) was referred to in the Herne Bay Urban District Council list of pleasure grounds as the East Cliff Recreation Ground. Contemporary reports of the various alternative entertainments on offer seem to indicate a certain amount of snobbery or class rivalry between the patrons. The military bands were highly regarded by the old guard who still held rosy memories of Herne Bay as a genteel watering place frequented by visitors who appeared for the summer season. The Fun Towers of the Jollity Boys with their tiered seats terraced into the slopes were the physical proof of the attractions of popular entertainers. This development of the alfresco entertainers, pierrots and jugglers was more to the taste of the day trippers who were increasingly coming to Herne Bay.

THIS PICTURE OF THE DOWNS was taken on Whit Monday 1911 shortly before 12.15 p.m. The band playing at the East Cliff Pavilion bandstand are the 19th Hussars under J.W. Tucker LRAM and the crowd gathered beyond are waiting for the first performance of the season by the scarlet coated Jollity Boys (see p. 126 top) under their manager Mr Arthur Vernon. Their performance was scheduled to start at the close of the band's performance.

EAST CLIFF BATHING CABINS on Saturday 22 June 1912, formally opened by the Chairman of the Council A.G. Iggulden JP. These two photographs show the successful and much extended scheme. In 1926 the council bought out the last private interest in bathing rights and by the early 1930s bathing machines had disappeared from the seafront. The cabins were designed by the council engineer Mr Palmer and constructed by the local contractor Griggs & Sons. Their very stripy appearance comes from the colour scheme which was as follows: the twenty ladies' cabins were green and white, the twenty gentlemen's cabins were blue and white, the ten family cabins (positioned in the centre) were red and white. Two pavilions provided accommodation for caretakers, ticket office and lavatories. The timber jetties which can be seen clearly in each picture were provided so that bathers could avoid the discomfort of the shingle.

HOT SEA BATHS WERE STILL BEING ADVERTISED on the side of the bath house below the sweeping tin roof, but the bathing machines have gone. With their wheels removed many of the old machines were called into service as changing cabins fixed on stilts above the beach. Frederick Holness was doing all he could to move with the times.

SEEN FROM THE EAST, THE FLAG-POLE marks the end of the stretch of beach under private control. Despite the public rights related to bathing, the construction of a platform and siting of cabins effectively closed off the beach. In 1926 the council bought out the remaining bathing rights that were still in private hands. In the foreground Mr Gammon with his boats for hire seems to have been pushed further along the beach.

THE SEVERE GALE of July 1924 swept through the cabins below the East Cliff, washing them back on to the parade. Even more damage was caused below Lane End at the St George's bathing station (see p. 13 bottom). In this picture, taken some years later, the changing cabins have gone. In the distance the council bathing facilities are expanding along the promenade, and the old bath house has been replaced by Cottew's Café. The owner, S.C. Cottew, lived next door in Sea View Cottage just as Frederick Holness had before him.

THE OFFICIAL TOWN GUIDE as published in 1927 by Herne Bay Urban District Council lists all the available options for bathing. Bathing from the beach beyond the town limits was available between sunrise and sunset. Between these points certain beaches could be used before 8.00 a.m. Bathing machines were said to be available at three bathing stations, and bathing cabins were available on the East and West beaches. Visitors could pitch their own tents below the East or West Cliffs. This picture taken around 1930 shows some of the council cabins as well as private tents. The charges for these cabins were 3d (1¼p) all ages before 8.30 a.m. After 8.30 adults 5d (2p), two or more persons together in one cabin 4d (1¾p) each person. As can be seen mixed bathing was permissible provided so called university costume was worn.

AFTER A GAP OF ALMOST THIRTY YEARS Herne Bay once again possessed a deep sea pier that could be used by steamers. This, the town's third pier, was built between 1896 and 1899, the pier pavilion at the shore end being retained. The new works were carried out by the contractor Head Wrightson to a design by E. Matheson. Complete with landing stage, the pier was 3,787 ft long and boasted a pierhead restaurant. The marquee on the widened section was used for band performances and entertainers. The tram that can be seen just beyond the tent was electric, and although not visible in this picture it normally ran with two open sided cars, one in front and one behind, when carrying passengers to and from the pier head.

FOLLOWING THE PURCHASE OF THE PIER by the local council in 1909 one of the first improvements carried out was the extension of the shore end, which was in part to allow the construction of a new pavilion. The official opening ceremony was carried out by the Lord Mayor of London (see p. 104 bottom). This photograph was almost certainly taken on a regatta day and the number of small boats in the water may indicate that one of the popular novelty races such as the duck hunt is in progress. The duck (a good swimmer was always chosen) was given a three minute start; the hunters, usually the winning boat from the Randan race, then had fifteen minutes to catch the duck. For maximum entertainment value this involved furious manoeuvring rather than straight line pursuit.

THE NEW PIER PAVILION which opened in 1910 was designed as a timber clad steel frame and built by Messrs W. Pattison Limited at £4,243. The joint architects were Percy J. Waldram of Charing Cross and Moscrop, Young and Glanfield of Bond Street. This visually lightweight building with its turrets, folding glazed screens and sun decks somehow captures the rather frivolous nature of a day at the seaside. In contrast, the tin box of the 1970s is a triumph of fire regulations over imagination.

WHEN THE PIER THEATRE BURNT DOWN in 1928 (see pp. 19 and 20) so many were impressed with the new open vista that a petition was circulated asking that the council should not erect a new building. This picture shows the pier entrance in 1929; the site is cleared and new paths laid but no real new scheme has been put in hand. The telephone box on the right, one of the first in the town is where Mr Cecil Baker raised the alarm with the brigade on the night of the fire.

THIS VIEW LOOKING EAST FROM THE PIER ENTRANCE in about 1912 is interesting for a number of reasons. The dark marks in the road clearly show the path of the water cart. This was provided to limit the nuisance of dusty roads and had been the butt of local jokes for many years. Some motor vehicles are evident but horse-drawn transport still dominates. The two chaps sitting on the barrow would probably have been offering their services to carry visitors' luggage to and from boarding houses and the station or pier. The new building on the left had been built to house the rocket life-saving equipment presented to the town in 1909 by Mr Duveen and Mr Renton (see p. 16). In the centre of the picture a band plays under a canvas roof; this particular arrangement was not often used and rarely appears in photographs.

THE NEW BANDSTAND WAS FORMALLY OPENED in 1924 and this view shows the new facility artistically framed by the supports of the flagstaff which had for so many years been the site for band performances (see p. 124 bottom). The reinforced concrete structure was designed by H. Kempton Dyson MI Struct E who was a specialist in reinforced concrete structures and a founder member of the Concrete Institute. This picture clearly shows the cantilevered roofs protecting the sun-decks and stage. The metal framework crossing the promenade carried sliding glazed screens which could be adjusted as necessary to screen the audience from the wind. Iron gates across the rear followed the line of the fence that had previously enclosed the tower gardens. At this first stage the new bandstand did not interrupt the line of the gardens.

LOOKING EAST ALONG THE TOWER GARDENS this view shows the situation that existed where some people preferred to listen to the band from chairs in the gardens rather than from within the new shelter. The through route along the line of the gardens was maintained but this was not to last. The picture was perhaps taken early in the season as council workmen are sorting out coloured bulbs for the overhead decorative lights.

THE NEW BANDSTAND was obviously very popular, not just for people listening to the bands but also for the sheltered seating that it provided overlooking the sea. The full width of the extended promenade is also made clear. A comparison with the picture at the top of p. 39 shows how the extra width was gained at the expense of the beach: the inside line of the promenade is on the line of the original fence to the Tower Gardens. The beach apparent here at the foot of the new wall was not to last for long. The thickening at the foot of the columns shows where cast-iron sleeves were installed to prevent the movement of shingle eroding the concrete. Imagine the outcry there would be today about the unprotected drop from the promenade to the beach below.

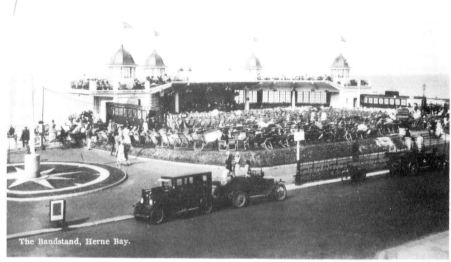

The Bandstand, Herne Bay.

AS THE NUMBER OF VISITORS WANTING TO SIT AND LISTEN to the bands grew then so did the demand for chairs. These needed to be accommodated in a situation where the council could collect their charges. Here we can see the raised seating area now pushing right back across the gardens. There was much argument in council meetings at the time concerning the desirability of having a chair over cool grass or hot concrete. If grass was originally used, as can be seen on the side banks, then it did not prove practical. To the left-hand side of the picture, railings can be seen along the edge of the promenade.

THE BANDSTAND, HERNE BAY.

THIS IS THE FINAL FORM OF THE BANDSTAND prior to enclosure with the seating area fully paved. The iron fence that started out on the seaward side of the original gardens has retreated back to the line of the pavement edge. The two lamps forming the gateway survived (without the fence) until the late 1940s.

THESE TWO PICTURES show almost the whole of the original Tower Gardens as they had evolved by the late 1920s. The original fence survives on the road side but the bandstand seating has pushed back across the gardens and is soon to be enclosed. The flagstaff remains in its original position. The dwarf wall with raised flower beds had first been approved by the council in 1924. This wall did stop a certain amount of water slopping back into the gardens during storms but the raised flower beds were never a great success. The elegant iron railings to the front gardens were removed in the salvage drive of January 1942.

THE FIRES OF THE LATE 1920s left the Council Surveyor B.J. Wormleighton with a number of headaches. As well as sorting out the pier entrance he had to deal with the disposal of the old Town Hall site and the move of the council offices into the refurbished YMCA building on the corner of Richmond Street (see p. 88 top). The pier site had taken some months to clear and the temporary works can be seen on p. 59. An elaborate scheme including shops, offices and toilets around an open rotunda was published in March 1929, but this proposal came to nothing when it was realized that the scheme could not be completed in time for the summer season. Many council members were also unhappy with the tendering procedures that made prices difficult to compare. This picture shows the very much reduced building that was erected. In time the central portion became a café, this building surviving until the early 1970s.

THIS DETAIL OF THE PIER ENTRANCE SEATING shows the style of the proposed grand scheme that was not to get further than the drawing board. The many curves and extensive use of pre-cast stonework are typical of the municipal seaside architecture of the period.

THE SEAFRONT seen here from St George's Terrace in about 1900. Root and Clarke's Dining Rooms were run by Mary Ann Root, whose husband John had been involved in business with the Oyster Company at Hampton until its financial collapse in the 1880s. Parallel to the catering business John Root developed a cycle hire and repair business, and in November 1894 John Clarke patented a jointing method for joining tubes in making cycle frames. As developments in motor cycles and tricycles moved forward so Root and Clarke were as advanced in their engineering as many other companies which are today household names. The cycle and motor car business grew, eventually to eclipse the catering, and the garage prospered and remained in the control of the Root family for a further two generations.

THIS IMPRESSIVE BUILDING on the seafront opposite the pier entrance was built in the 1830s. The Pier Hotel as it was known was aimed at serving the steamer passengers landing at the first pier. The hotel was never a success financially, and the building changed hands many times before becoming a children's home. Remembered by many people as St Anne's Home, the building was demolished in the 1960s to make way for flats. This photograph dates from around 1908. The garden to the right-hand side of the picture belonged to Pier Villa, the home of Captain F.W. Wacher of the fire brigade.

ST GEORGE'S PARADE seen from in front of the pier entrance in about 1905. The Kent Tavern on the corner has just come into the ownership of Ernest Foreman Wheeler, who also continued to run his well established oyster saloon next door. In stark contrast to today this parade contained a post office, library and reading rooms, tea rooms and a gentleman's club. The last building before Lane End is St George's Baths and the bathing machines for the west bathing station can be seen on the beach below. At this time the business was run by Frederick Ashwell. The motor cycle with the splended wickerwork side car may well belong to the photographer.

ST GEORGE'S BATHS. This bathing station effectively marked the western limit of the town until about 1905. Lane End swung up to Sea Street with only isolated buildings among open fields, and brickworks to the west. A common complaint from visitors who had bought plots on the West Cliff was that while the absentee owners were not able to keep an eye on things the locals allowed their goats to eat shrubs and hedges planted on the plots.

THE WEST CLIFF. In this picture more building development is apparent although there are still less than ten houses actually facing the sea between Lane End and the George Hotel. There are plenty of bathing tents on the beach, reflecting the increasingly relaxed attitude to bathing.

THE COASTGUARD STATION stood on the top of the beach below Albany Drive; this building was demolished in 1905 to allow the promenade to be extended west from Lane End. At least seven men were stationed here with one officer. Apart from their official duties some of the men built and hired out frames for bathing tents on the beach between Lane End and the station. Beyond the jurisdiction of the town beadle the officer in charge may have turned a blind eye to this activity. Although we know the names of all the coastguards, individuals have so far escaped identification (the man with the moustache also appears on p. 94).

THE PROPRIETOR C.N. HOLNESS used this photograph to illustrate his advert for the St George's Baths in the 1923 Official Town Guide. Holness was offering pleasant and safe bathing with expert attention, up-to-date cabins, diving stations and rafts. The baths just off the picture to the right were open from 7.00 a.m. with hot or cold fresh or sea water. Judging by the size of the crowd and the bunting this picture was almost certainly taken on a regatta day.

THE WEST BEACH photographed around 1906. The promenade has been extended west from Lane End but no railings have been installed. This beach was divided into three sections for bathing purposes: from Lane End the first 338 yd west were available to male and female bathers (with screen or shelter), the next 338 yd were male only (without screen or shelter) and the last section of 395 yd was male and female again (with screen or shelter), all these categories applying from sunrise to sunset. Quite why males should be allowed to undress without the use of screens between the beaches where such screens were compulsory is a bit of a mystery. The penalty for a breach of the bye-laws was a hefty five pound fine.

THE WEST BEACH seen here from the pier in the early 1930s. The bathing station at St George's Baths is still in full swing with bathers using the rafts and diving platforms. Boatmen are busy hiring out small rowing boats as well as offering motor boat trips around the bay.

THE WEST CLIFF seen here looking west from just beyond Lane End in the mid-1920s appears not much different to the same view today. The concrete bathing cabins just below the bottom right-hand corner of this picture had recently been completed. The West Cliff shelter in the middle distance (now the headquarters of the Heron Angling Club) had been opened in October 1923. A deposit of twenty-five pounds with small weekly payments would still secure a new house in several of the roads running up off Western Esplanade.

WESTERN ESPLANADE beyond Selsea Avenue did not benefit from the extension of the promenade wall. In this picture, also from the mid-1920s, the beach huts are beginning to assume a fairly standard form although not yet organized into a formal line. The council rule that huts must be removed from the beach in the winter was originally used as a device to control the form of the huts themselves. This was not a rule that many owners observed. The original East Cliff bandstand (see p. 53) can be clearly seen in its role as a shelter.

SECTION FOUR

Buildings

*Shops – Garages – Farms – Town Hall – Hotels – Public Houses
Churches – Street Scenes*

THE SITE OF THIS FLORAL NURSERY AND FRUITERER is now known as 32/34 High Street, the premises of Cocketts Mattresses Ltd showrooms and workshops. P. Dilnot, seen holding a potted palm, started business here around 1909. He followed G.H. Stent (Stent had nursery grounds in Canterbury Road to the north of Spencer Road). Before Stent the Cade brothers ran a similar business from the early 1890s. When this picture was taken around 1910 the Dilnots lived behind the premises in Brunswick Cottage, Brunswick Square. Despite the large sign across the roof, there is no apparent record of the business having a branch at Canterbury. By 1940 more than half a century of connection with flowers, seeds, fruit and vegetables ended with the arrival of an upholsterer Harry Saunders. The terrace of houses to the west of this property was originally known as Sunflower Villas, and relics of this early name remain in the form of ornate metal sunflower finials to the front roofs.

Opposite:

THE NAME RIDOUT can be found among some of the earliest records of the town. This rather battered photograph shows their premises in William Street between Webbs the jeweller and the Windmill Café. The lettering and signs are more examples of the work of Billy Smeed; in this case they are all painted direct on to the rendered elevation. The shop window displays dozens of picture post cards. An example of the sort of poster work carried out by their print works can be seen on p. 123.

THE PROUD SHOP OWNER STANDING IN THE DOORWAY is Sidney Albert Brown, his wife Daisy stands on his left, and the second lady is Daisy's sister Agnes Butler. Above the open sliding sash windows the shopfront is superbly decorated for Christmas 1912; they had opened a year or two earlier. Daisy was the inspiration for the business as her family had been involved in the greengrocery trade elsewhere. Sidney's father was a local builder with premises in William Street next to the parish church (now an insurance broker's premises). The Browns retired in the early 1950s but the shop still trades as a florist.

THIS SUPERB PHOTOGRAPH SHOWS A DAIRY on the corner of Station Road and Brunswick Square. The premises had previously been a butcher's, and today the shop is still recognizable but has for many years been in the hands of Welch and Sons the undertakers. The hand delivery carts are milk prams, so called because of their similarity with domestic prams of the period. The polished churns each held about sixteen gallons (75 litres), and the milk was served from a tap into customers' own cans. The cans along the side of the pram could be left with customers and collected the next day. The development of milk bottling plant made these prams redundant and some were converted to carry crates. In the early years of doorstep bottle deliveries it was not unknown (although quite illegal) for roundsmen to carry milk with them in order to refill some of the bottles collected earlier in the round.

Opposite:

NO SHORTAGE OF STOCK HERE. The Domestic Bazaar Co. Ltd was one of several shops along the seafront selling cheap seaside souvenirs. Around 1910 most of the china ornaments came from the continent; they carried curious town coats of arms of dubious pedigree, and most seem to combine a heron and the clock tower against an orange or red background. The photographs decorating the huge range of objects in the left-hand window may well have originated from the Tower Studio next door. At this time Frederick Christian Palmer ran the studio and was responsible for many of the photographs in this book. The Sea View Café and Restaurant to the other side was run by Giovanni Mazzoleni; he also had the restaurant at the Pier Theatre.

THE CREAMERIES' PREMISES at 176 Mortimer Street had been used for the same business for some thirty years before the names of Woollard and Cottew came together over the door. James Woollard followed J. Gore into No. 94 (later 176) Mortimer Street in 1915. In 1911 the Cottew brothers were trading in Station Road, Promenade Central and at the Ridgeway Dairy, Mortimer Street. In this picture the carefully polished motor van takes centre stage, while behind the van can be seen a milk pram originally developed to carry a churn prior to bottled milk deliveries (see picture opposite). The name boards above the shop fascia, although painted out, can still be seen in place today. The building's flank wall in East Street still carries the faded remains of a painted advertisement for Creameries Dairy Café, the lettering being painted over an idealized pastoral scene.

THOMAS BROWN CLARK traded as a baker from these premises in William Street from 1913 until 1937. His father and grandfather were both millers, and as a boy Thomas worked for his father William in the family mill at Eastry. These premises now house a building society.

THE YORKSHIRE BAKERY AT NO. 8 THE HIGH STREET has retained virtually all its original shopfront dating from the 1920s. In the earlier years of the century No. 8 was a Temperance Hotel known as the Waverley. The bakery was started by a Swiss lady but the business has been a Turner family concern since the late 1920s. This photograph was taken in the early evening probably to show to best advantage the latest thing in illuminated shop signs. Today the electrics have long since vanished but the original name can still be seen replacing the script on the lower fascia. The sweet shop to the right offering freshly made fudge for 2s (10p) per pound was the confectionery department of Cowell's the grocers two doors to the left at No. 12.

QUEEN'S MOTOR GARAGE, CANTERBURY ROAD. This splendid line-up of machinery shows practically the full range of models available from Standard Cars in 1932. From left to right the vehicles are as follows: Standard Twenty Special Saloon (6 cylinder 2552 cc); Standard Sixteen Special Saloon (6 cylinders 2054 cc); Standard Big Nine or Big Twelve (both share the same bodywork); Standard Little Twelve (6 cylinder 1337 cc); Standard Little Nine Saloon (4 cylinder 1006 cc). The sports car at the end is an Avon bodied Standard Sixteen fixed head coupé with dickey seat. In standard form the Little Nine saloon on Dunlop tyres and with safety glass all round would have cost £155. The dearest model, the Twenty Special on the left, would have run out at £355. The young man in the centre of the picture (wearing plus-fours) is Bill Buck (the son of '& Son'). Bill served with the air force in both world wars, and many people in the town will remember the motorboat *Swordfish* which Bill ran for many years from the beach to the west of the pier.

BLACKWELL AND SONS MOTOR BODY BUILDERS. This photograph is typical of a type that many small firms had produced for publicity purposes to show off their latest product or new premises. In this case it is the only evidence that this firm were involved in this particular business. In 1909 A.J. Blackwell was living in Rose Cottage, Richmond Street and managing the Richmond Forge Company in Hanover Street. By 1925 A.J. was working with his son as a general smith from premises in Beach Street just off the High Street (A.J. is the man with his foot on the running board). This yard was on the north side of the High Street just below Underdown Street (now Bank Street).

'THE CABIN' SWEET SHOP WAS IN MARINE PARADE, the last business premises before Canterbury Road. In this photograph the name on the fascia. J.A. Richardson has been crossed out. Mrs M. Howard took the business from about 1927. On the evening of Saturday 28 October Mr Howard was attacked by a thief armed with a large air-pistol. Although nothing was taken Mr Howard was knocked to the ground, and his assailant dropped the weapon on the shop floor before fleeing.

THE SIGNWRITER BILLY SMEED did not have to walk far to complete this job at The Stores on the corner of Bank Street and Mortimer Street. This dog-eared photograph was one of two (the other is on p. 73) that spent their first forty years or so pinned up in Smeed's studio workshop behind the Writery at No. 3 Bank Street. The shopfront of Smeed's premises in Bank Street remains today as a classic example of the gilded and acid cut glass work that was once common on shopfronts. Billy Smeed made the fascia, assisted by a young Ernest Davey, at a workshop off Beach Street. Mr Davey joined Smeed as an apprentice in 1928, and he once explained to me that Smeed thought the complicated reverse work on glass was not worthwhile. Once he had completed his own signs (to a very high standard) he never took on similar work for clients.

EAST HILL. The earliest visitors to Herne Bay would have viewed the sea from this spot where the road from Canterbury met the bay. With the exception of The Ship at the foot of the hill the buildings have obviously changed considerably since the days before Sir Henry Oxenden's little township. In this photograph taken in the late 1920s the corner newsagents was owned by Hugh Latimer. The house next door to Latimer's is now a restaurant. The view is much the same today, the pavements still have granite kerbs although the cobbled gutters are full of tarmac and yellow lines.

THIS SADDLERS WAS AT CANTERBURY HOUSE in Mortimer Street (now No. 56 just east of Beach Street). The name Rowden is more usually associated locally with farming. This business would seem to have been in a good position. The Tower Hotel and Victoria Hotel each had stables within a stone's throw and Wacher and Co. had their stables just down the road in Telford Street. Wacher's advertising for 1903 lists pair and single horse carriages of every description, omnibuses, cabs, brakes, pony carriages, landaus, victorias and dog carts, all for hire. The photograph is dated 12 February 1903 and has the name F.E. Brown written on the back – perhaps the young man in the doorway is Mr Brown. The number of whips on display and the type of harness perhaps indicate the importance of horse-drawn vehicles rather than saddle horses at the time. By 1909 the saddler had gone and John Cullins was catering for Shanks's pony as a bootmaker.

FRANCIS GEORGE WINCH traded as a butcher from No. 13 Mortimer Street between 1900 and 1911. The premises were to remain in the same trade for many years. In more recent times No. 13 (now No. 138) has seen service as part of the local labour exchange. Although the shop window has seen many alterations, some original details seen in this photograph have survived. At the time of writing these notes the steel hanging rail can still be seen above the fascia. Perhaps more surprisingly the decorative ceramic tile head seen level with the window transom on the left-hand side can still be seen looking out at the street through eighty years of gloss paint. The large quantity of meat on display probably indicates that this photograph was taken just before Christmas.

G.W. LANE WAS TRADING AS A BOOKSELLER AND STATIONER from the building to the left of this photograph (then No. 27 Mortimer Street) as early as 1909. This lean-to building was constructed over the access to Rogers and Anderson's coalyard which was between the original shop and the Congregational church. In the foreground the granite setts (now obscured by the concrete blocks of the pedestrianization scheme) show where the horse-drawn coal carts used to turn across the pavement into the yard. Coal barges were unloaded at the clock tower slipway at hours convenient to the tides and barge owners rather than when other people slept. The creaking of carts and noise of horses' hooves on the road was a constant source of complaint for people living in Market Street and Mortimer Street on the route between the beach and the yard. In 1922 the publishers Cassell's ran a window dressing competition, and this photograph shows the display that won second prize for Lanes. Can you imagine how many times you would have to feature the sponsor's name to win first prize?

PARSONAGE FARMHOUSE looks as if it should be surrounded by orchards deep in the folds of rural Kent. In fact this building stood just south of the North Kent Railway line some 100 yd east of Canterbury Road. The farmhouse and its outbuildings were cleared for the development of Parsonage Road and Herne Bay Court. This picture shows the south elevation of the house with members of the Gore family posing on the front lawn. The style of dress indicates a date around 1865, making this one of the earliest photographs in this collection.

THIS VIEW LOOKING UP WILLIAM STREET was taken by the Canterbury photographer Craik (who did not open his Herne Bay shop at 55 William Street until 1892). The bunting and flags are probably part of the 1887 Jubilee celebrations. The town marked this year with a number of suitable gestures. 1887 saw the opening of the Tower Gardens on the seafront, the New Schools in Kings Road and new Local Board Offices in the High Street. The ornate fountain on the seafront, although presented as a Jubilee memorial, was not formally handed over to the town until September 1888. In the light of its current neglected state it is interesting to read that Mr Farley, speaking on behalf of the Local Board, undertook to 'maintain the gift in its fullest efficiency'.

THIS BUILDING on the corner of William Street and the High Street was built for a private company in 1859. The builder was C.S. Welby, whose son was later to figure in the building's history (see p. 18). In 1873 it was purchased to serve as the Town Hall, and the authorities spent some £1,500 on repair and renovations in 1904 and 1905. The important role of such a building as a central meeting place for the town for anything from a serious political debate to an amateur theatre company's farce is a need that has not been fully met in Herne Bay since 1925. Every town should have a Town Hall.

THIS PHOTOGRAPH OF THE ROYAL HOTEL was posted as a Christmas card in 1904. The building at the corner of William Street and the seafront had previously been used as a surgery by Dr A. Rawlings, and at that time (1897) it was known as The Lodge. In 1900 the Royal Hotel sign appeared with the name of James Stephen White over the door. White had been a member of the local board since 1888 and in 1902 was vice-chairman of the HBUDC. White was involved with a number of licensed premises, and before taking the Royal he had been at the New Dolphin for some years. Jimmy White as he was known was also a long standing member of the fire brigade and can be seen in this capacity on p. 22.

THE STATION BUILDINGS SEEN FROM STATION ROAD. The style of dress and horse-drawn carriages indicate a date of around 1910 for this picture. For some hundred years after the arrival of the railway the station marked the narrowest part of the town where open country reached within half a mile of the seafront. Visitors walking down Station Road to the sea before the First World War would find the area to their right undeveloped between the Grand Hotel and Kings Road with only a handful of buildings on the left-hand side. The poorly drained area north of Spencer Road that was to become the Memorial Park was frequently referred to in the local press as a disgrace to the town.

THE ROSE INN, MORTIMER STREET. James Heavens used this photographic postcard to carry a Christmas message in December 1911. Good wishes went from him and his family who are presumably all gathered in the doorway. The painted lettering on the flank wall is a particularly good example of the sign writer's skill at achieving a three dimensional effect without the expense of individually cut and raised letters.

SEA VIEW SQUARE WAS PART OF THE REDEVELOPMENT of the mill field site on the seafront following the mill's demolition in 1878. This photograph shows the row of houses built across the end of the square Nos 4, 5 and 6. As can be seen, these were known as Saint Saviours Grange, Home of Rest for Women and Girls, and the home was run by an order of nuns. For many years the manageress was Sister Alice Mary; the figure in the apron may well be the matron Miss Smith. In the 1950s the nuns moved out to a new Colt house built at the top of Mickleburgh Hill, and Nos 4, 5 and 6 reverted to being separate dwellings.

THIS IMPOSING BUILDING ON THE CORNER OF CANTERBURY ROAD and Charles Street was for many years the home of Miss Watson's school for young ladies. In 1912 Herne Bay boasted thirteen such establishments catering for the 'daughters of gentlemen'. By the 1920s when this photograph was taken the property had become a small private hotel, and the building has suffered mixed fortunes since. Along with the attached buildings in Charles Street it has been a private club, a restaurant and latterly private flats.

BELLE VUE, on the corner of Richmond Street and the seafront, was originally built as a hotel. Prior to its purchase by the YMCA it was run as a private girls' school by Miss King. The premises were refurbished by C.W. Welby with accommodation provided for seventy to eighty guests.

THE CHILDREN PLAYING IN AVENUE ROAD faced little danger from traffic in 1912. The sign on the White Horse carries the name Ash's; in 1920 Ash's Brewery merged with East Kent Brewers to form Ash's East Kent Brewery Limited. In 1925 this concern was taken over by Jude and Hanbury, who in turn were taken over by Whitbread in 1929.

EVERSLEY VILLAS, SOUTH ROAD. This terrace looked out over the Herne Bay Tennis Ground between Queen's Gardens and Victoria Park, one of Herne Bay's once open squares. These houses, built for around £200 (excluding the cost of the site), are typical of the speculative development responsible for the growth of the town in the 1880s and 1890s.

ST JOHN'S CHURCH IN BRUNSWICK SQUARE was built on a site which was the gift of Sir Henry Oxenden. The foundation stone was laid by the Lord Mayor of London on Thursday 28 July 1898, and the nave was completed in the following year by the local builder A.S. Ingleton. This photograph dates from around 1904 and shows toothed brickwork exposed on the corner of the building; this was in preparation for a bell tower which was illustrated on the architect's original 1898 drawings but which was never built. In 1973, faced with falling congregations and income, the church commissioners chose to retain the parish church in William Street. Despite considerable local opposition St John's was demolished to make way for an old people's home.

THIS AERIAL PHOTOGRAPH taken in the early 1930s shows how far development had reached to the east of the town. New houses have not quite surged over the brow of the hill at Mickleburgh Avenue, and cows still graze peacefully in the open fields between Dence Park, Beltinge Road and Reculver Road. In the foreground the left-hand convalescent home has now been demolished and the neat vegetable garden at the rear now has a crop of houses. The large iron gates of the original home can still be seen in Reculver Road. They have been re-erected rather like an ancient trophy in front of a very average replacement building.

THE BROADWAY, seen here from opposite Ridgeway Cliff, was made up in the early 1930s. The new houses sit in a patchwork of undeveloped but tidy plots with isolated cottages and rows of houses relating to the earlier brickworks. This gradual development has ensured that many roads on the West Cliff contain houses from almost every decade of the century; a rich pattern which by definition cannot be repeated.

THE GIRDLERS in Beacon Hill is remembered by many people in the town as a private girls' school. This photograph dating from about 1914 shows the building as a private hotel before it became a school. The flat-roofed ivy clad building in the middle distance is the billiard room at the end of the garden of St Malo further up the hill, this building is now a private residence. The Girdlers is a residential home for the elderly.

THE HOTEL ST GEORGE was known as the St George's Cliff Family and Commercial Hotel in the early years of the century. This hotel and the coastguard station (see p. 67 bottom) were the only substantial buildings on the front west of Lane End. In their advertising the various owners have always made much of the fine views available from the hotel's elevated position. This picture shows the building as originally built (a rear extension was soon added). At this time the hotel boasted a tennis court, bowling green and putting green. The tower on the corner complete with turret was a popular feature of large houses in the town and other good examples can still be seen on the East Cliff (see picture above).

THIS IS ONE OF THE VERY FEW PICTURES IN THIS BOOK not taken by a local photographer and is a view looking down Mortimer Street taken early in the 1930s. In those days street parking was obviously not a problem. William Street car park was still a grassy square where good quality club cricket was played through the summer months. A third-class ticket from London would cost a visitor 10s 6d (52p). For people who wanted to move to the town freehold detached bungalows were available in Bognor Drive at £550.

THE TOP END of Mortimer Street was probably photographed for the company Valentines on the same day as the picture above. On the left Winch the butcher is still trading although he has moved shop twice since he was at the premises shown on p. 81. Woolworth's on the right is trading as the 3d and 6d (1¾p and 2½p) stores. The cameraman is standing within yards of the first building plots that had been set out off the Canterbury Road some one hundred years earlier.

SECTION FIVE

Events

Torpedoes – Whale – Army Visits – Empire Day – Royal Visits
Official Openings – Sea Baptism – Coronation Celebrations

JAMES FURNEAUX left home for his usual morning bathe at 6.00 a.m. on Wednesday 20 September 1905. No doubt to his surprise he noticed something bright on the beach, which turned out to be a torpedo. James rushed back to tell his father, Chief Officer Furneaux of the Herne Bay Coastguards. The torpedo was a Whitehead type complete with calcium light still burning. On Thursday afternoon the Admiralty sent torpedo boat No. 77 to Herne Bay, the coastguards towed the torpedo out and it was lifted aboard. James Furneaux is the lad in the cap standing behind the torpedo which seems to have been lashed to some kind of boat launching trolley. This particular photograph hung in the bar of the Kent Tavern for many years.

ANOTHER TORPEDO WAS CAUSING EXCITEMENT on the beach in 1912. This one was not washed up but was towed in by Mr A. Sprules and two anglers who had found it while fishing in a boat off Herne Bay near 'the channel'. By trade Mr Sprules was a chimney sweep living at 53 Avenue Road. It seems likely that he is the man with the large moustache standing in front of the torpedo. On his cap he is wearing the badge of the Herne Bay Angling Association. The torpedo was towed onto the beach to the east of the pier on Wednesday evening (24 July) where it apparently attracted large crowds, as did the Navy launch which came to collect it on the Thursday. For the technically minded the weapon was probably an 18 in Whitehead RGF type V or VI. The name DORIS stencilled on the nose tells us where it came from. *Doris* was a Second Class Cruiser of 5,600 tons built by Vickers at Barrow in 1896.

THIS PHOTOGRAPH WAS TAKEN IN 1948 so really it is too late for this collection. However, I have included it for two reasons: firstly, small children that have seen it seem amazed that anything so big could be swimming in the sea off Herne Bay. Secondly, it fits in so well with the torpedos. The whale was washed up at Hampton on 19 August 1948, and died as the tide receded. On the Saturday morning council workmen removed the carcass for burial at Broomfield dump. The small boy in the raincoat and cap standing behind the tail fluke is the young David Chalk, son of Harry who ran the boating lakes further along Hampton Pier Avenue. In more recent years David has won most of the angling trophies on offer at the local clubs. David is one of the handful of people to have won the HBAA Championship Shield on more than one occasion (see p. 118 bottom).

IN MAY 1905 THE ROYAL EAST KENT YEOMANRY were encamped for annual training at Ramsgate and on Monday 29 May they visited Herne Bay. A camping ground was provided for them east of Canterbury Road and south of Mickleburgh Hill. This picture shows the troops approaching what is now the busy roundabout at the foot of Mickleburgh Hill. Mr & Mrs Miller at the Queen's Hotel decorated their building with festoons of oak leaves (using the theme of Oak Apple Day) and flags and bunting were strung across the road to Commercial Buildings opposite. On this occasion all the street decorations were erected on the Monday morning as this work was thought unsuitable for the Sabbath.

THE TOWN HALL WAS ALSO DECORATED for the visit of the Yeomanry. In the background of this picture the fire brigade can be seen with an arch made out of ladders across the road outside their headquarters. It is difficult to imagine why canvas buckets were seen as such decorative objects; however the brigade gets ten out of ten for effort (see p. 105). The carriage in the picture was the last of five heading the procession, the passengers being J.S. White JP, Chairman of the Council, P.E. Iggulden, Vice Chairman, J. Jubb, the Clerk, and F.H. Wilbee JP. The man sitting next to the driver is Adolphus Boorman the beadle.

IN AUGUST 1909 THE SECOND LONDON DIVISIONAL Royal Engineers came to camp at Herne Bay for the second time. They arrived at the railway station on Sunday afternoon (1 August) and this view shows the men and horses at the railway station. The gentleman in the bowler hat (bottom left) is probably station master Mr McIntosh who was responsible for the disembarkation arrangements. There was no official reception although a crowd gathered at the station including Mr N. Rowden Snr JP, Chairman of the Council. During their two week stay the troops were entertained in the town with special concerts and sports. As this was the busiest time of the year for the town one such concert for 400 men was actually held at the pierhead.

THE ACTUAL CAMP SITE was to the north of Beltinge Village and east of Sea View Road. This picture shows Colonel Clifford marching his men to church for the Sunday Service. The building under construction on the left is Coombe Cottage (now on the corner of Cliff Avenue). During their stay the men built a pontoon bridge across Broomfield pond. The spectacle of all this activity provided considerable entertainment for the villagers and visitors who turned up to watch in some numbers. The engineers also linked their camp, Broomfield and the town by telegraph and telephone.

THE FLAGSTAFF WAS ALSO USED AS AN ASSEMBLY POINT outside the holiday season. 21 October 1905 was a very cold day but people still began to gather on the front from about 10.00 a.m. This was Nelson's Day, the centenary of his death and this picture shows the crowd on the pavement in front of Belle Vue School. No doubt the headmistress Miss King has given the girls strict instructions on behaviour. Those on the balcony are heavily dressed with coats, scarves and fur collars, and some like the ladies on the pavement are using fur muffs. The streets were decorated with flags and bunting. Thanks to the efforts of Chief Officer Furneaux of the coastguards, the flagstaff carried the famous signal 'England expects every man will do his duty'.

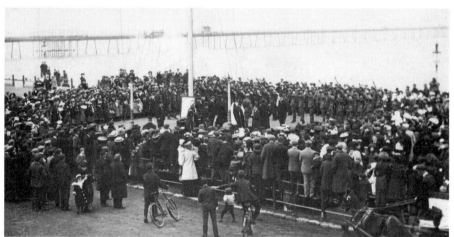

NELSON'S DAY 1905. Soon after 12 noon the salute was fired by the local volunteers. The two portable organs at the base of the flagstaff were used for playing the national anthem. The fireman with his polished brass helmet is Mr J.S. White JP, in his official capacity as Lieutenant of the Fire Brigade. The figure in the surplice is the Revd T.B. Watkins.

EMPIRE DAY, 24 MAY 1908. 'All parties, all classes, all creeds united in paying homage to that symbol of the British Empire the Union Jack'. This celebration was organized by a committee and the members of the Herne Bay Navy and Army Veterans Association. The united service was to commence at the flagstaff at 4.00 p.m. and various groups assembled opposite the pier entrance. In this view we can see the New College Cadet Corps, the Fire Brigade under Captain F.W. Wacher and the Boys' Brigade with Captain T.F. Ridout in command. Yet to get themselves lined up are the Coastguard, the Volunteers, the Veterans and the Ambulance Corps.

THIS CROWD IS ASSEMBLED ROUND THE FLAGSTAFF to celebrate Empire Day 1909. The service was held on Sunday 23 May although Empire Day proper was on the 24th. The signal flags spell out the words 'Empire Day'. To the right of the open area is a roped enclosure for the children of the Sunday schools and private schools. The ring of bandsmen around the flagstaff are the Excelsior Brass Band under bandmaster Fairall. The temperature was reported to be in the eighties and many of the men are wearing straw boaters with the ladies in blouses and broad brimmed hats.

JULY 24 1907 WAS AN EXCITING DAY for many people in Herne Bay. Princess Louise Duchess of Argyll, daughter of the late Queen Victoria and sister to King Edward VII was coming to the town to open a new extension to the Passmore Edwards Railway Men's Convalescent Home at Blacksole. The official street decorations were under the direction of F.W.J. Palmer, the council surveyor. Local businessmen and householders vied with each other decorating their properties along the procession route. This picture shows the junction of Station Road and the High Street. The venetian masts were twenty-two feet high and decorated with bracken and flowers and the 'Welcome' banner was lettered in white on a red background. The large decoration seemingly suspended above the shop awning on the left is a large crown formed in glass fairy lights which was the work of the shop owner John Henry Whitchurch. The building covered in posters on the next corner is the Pier Hotel livery stables.

THE VIEW LOOKING BACK UP STATION ROAD FROM the seafront on the same day shows the mass of greenery used by the Pier Hotel and Messrs Root & Clarke to form an archway between their premises. Although to one side of the intended route, St Annes Home, to the right of the picture, was also decorated with flags and bunting.

THE MOST EXTRAVAGANT DECORATION was probably this arch at the foot of Mickleburgh Hill. This was the work of George Miller, licensee of the Queens Hotel. The arch was composed of beech, hazel and oak. The message 'A Loyal Welcome' featured the arms of the Duke of Argyll in the centre. The hotel itself which was then a relatively new building, having opened in 1901, was also decorated with greenery, flags and 'symbols of loyalty and patriotism'.

IT WAS AGREED BY THE COUNCIL that the local Volunteers would form a guard of honour at the Town Hall. Refreshments were to be provided for the men at not more than 1s (5p) per head. This view shows the men marching along the seafront after assembling at Richmond Street along with other men from Birchington and Margate. If the clock tower was showing the correct time they had about five minutes to get round to the Town Hall.

THIS PICTURE SHOWS THE PRINCESS DRIVING along the seafront with her mounted escort of Dragoon Guards. Whoever supplied the flags and bunting must have done quite well out of this visit. The timber venetian masts supporting the flags were supplied and erected by Messrs Ingleton Brothers, local builders, whose offices were at Garibaldi Terrace in the High Street. Ingleton offered the council two options: poles painted red white and blue at 1s 3d (8p) each, and poles painted a single colour red or white or blue at 1s 1d (5½p). They went for the cheaper price which was inclusive of carting and fixing.

THIS WAS THE SCENE AT THE TOWN HALL in the High Street minutes before the arrival of the Princess. Lieutenant E.W. Turner has got his Volunteers lined up opposite the Town Hall after marching them round from the seafront. Police Sergeant Lampkin seems to be clarifying a few last minute instructions. Somewhere in the background little Miss Aline Hogbin, daughter of councillor Hogbin, was probably practising her curtsy ready for presenting a bouquet of roses to the Princess.

A FINE BODY OF MEN. The date of this picture must be July 1907 and the group may well be the committee of councillors that was responsible for all the arrangements for the royal visit. As the picture cannot have been taken on the Wednesday of the visit, a good possibility is that they are dressed up ready for the rehearsal held the previous Saturday. This is one of a series of more than thirty photographs published by Palmer as souvenirs of the visit.

ON 3 AUGUST 1910 THE LORD MAYOR OF LONDON SIR JOHN KNILL came to Herne Bay to open the New Pier Pavilion (see p. 59 top). The Lord Mayor, Lady Mayoress and the Sheriffs came to the town by train and then processed round the town in carriages. Their route shows us which parts of the town were thought worth showing off at the time. They drove down Station Road to the High Street, up the High Street, left into William Street and right into Mortimer Street, on to Canterbury Road and left up Beltinge Road, left into Belle Vue Road and left down Beacon Hill, then right down East Cliff Hill to the seafront. This photograph shows the Mayor's coach pulled by four greys about to pass the Clock Tower. In all there were fifteen coaches and no less than seven Kentish mayors attended. The town must have made a favourable impression as the following year these important visitors stayed at Herne Bay when Sir John was recuperating following an illness.

THE TOWN ONCE AGAIN HUNG WITH FLAGS AND BUNTING in July 1913 when another royal visit was in prospect. The scale of decorations did not however compare with 1907. Princess Henry of Battenberg was coming to the town. Representing Queen Alexandra she was to open the King Edward VII Memorial Hall and visit the Queen Victoria Memorial Cottage Hospital. As on previous similar occasions open horse-drawn carriages (sixteen in total) carried the various dignitaries around the town en route from the station to the pier. This photograph shows the Princess travelling from the pier to the East Cliff by motor car. The Princess can be seen turning back for a second look at the amazing arch formed by the Herne Bay Fire Brigade.

ON THURSDAY 11 NOVEMBER 1920 at 11.00 a.m. a maroon exploded by the Clock Tower. Two minutes' silence on this the second anniversary of the Armistice was observed absolutely. Traffic stopped in the streets, motors were turned off and all business and trading ceased. At the side of the Town Hall in William Street the end of two minutes was marked by the playing of the last post. This duty was carried out by four members of the 1st Herne Bay Scouts. Patrol leader H. Boswell and F. Wilkinson, Corporal J. Ells and Scout G. Greenhead were under the direction of Corpl-Drummer F. Hayward late of the Buffs. An address was read by Mr H.W. Hall, Chairman of the Council.

PEACE CELEBRATIONS, 19 July 1919 saw Herne Bay celebrating peace following the Armistice of November 1918; this section of spectators is waiting to the east of the flagstaff. The salute was to be taken by Lieut Col J.H. Lang Sims OBE, N. Rowden the Chairman of the Council, Mr H.W. Hall the Vice Chairman, and representatives of all the town's churches were also in attendance. The men in front of the dais with white covers on their peaked caps are Navy and Army Veterans.

THE BROTHERHOOD OF CHEERFUL SPARROWS was dedicated to raising money locally for a number of worthy causes. This particular occasion is the dedication of a new ambulance for the Herne Bay division of the Order of St John. In the centre of the photograph is Canon N.H. Harding Jolly MA, vicar of Herne Bay, and to the right holding his hat is Mr W.H. Randell President of the Brotherhood of Cheerful Sparrows. The officer in uniform is Mr E.A. Richards Commissioner of No. 8 District (of which Herne Bay was part), on the far left is the Revd W.R. Lloyd of the Congregational church, and next to him is Mr H.J. Carr of the Baptist church. The vehicle was supplied by Messrs Chase of the High Street Garage. The 24 h.p. Ford chassis was extended to a 123 in wheelbase, the coachwork was produced locally but newspaper reports of the time do not tell us who carried it out. This was the town's second ambulance. The photograph was taken outside the parish church in William Street on Sunday 15 February 1931. After many years of organizing fund raising events W.H. Randell died in April 1933.

ON WEDNESDAY EVENING 24 JULY 1929 people on the seafront were able to observe an unusual diversion from the normal alfresco entertainments. The local assembly of the Elim Foursquare Gospel Church held a baptism on the beach below Lane End. There were eight women and two men candidates. The gentleman on the right with the braces is Pastor E. Davies of Canterbury. The total immersion is being carried out by Pastor William C. Horton of the local assembly. At the time this group usually met at the YMCA hut in Mortimer Street. I suspect that there was considerable disbelief in various playgrounds when some of the children told their friends what they had seen at the seaside.

THE SEAFRONT HAD BEEN DECORATED WITH ELECTRIC LIGHTS in the 1920s; however the Coronation of 1937 provided the excuse for a far more elaborate scheme to be installed. This included the use of neon on the Clock Tower. The work was carried out under the direction of B.J. Wormleighton the council surveyor and the scheme extended from Lane End to the King's Hall. Other celebrations included a Coronation Pageant. The programme for this event cost 6d (2½p) and lists sixty-six different local organizations that provided players for the finalé. The pageant itself was in six episodes, each representing Herne Bay as seen at the time of coronations since 1821.

THE THEME OF ROYALTY WAS EVIDENT EVERYWHERE and the council offices carried a huge royal crown outlined in lights of the national colours. The shields which could be seen mounted on the lamp standards were the work of W. Smeed. The boy scouts, guides and boys' brigade were all involved in the pageant; they also made 500 torches which were used in a torchlight procession from each end of the town to the pier pavilion where there was a grand party followed by a fireworks display.

THE MOST STRIKING LIGHTING SCHEME which could be seen from all over the district was the water tower. This illumination was designed by Messrs Cutler, Robert & Co. Fixed 200 ft above sea level the crown was ten feet high and made up of more than 400 lamps. The 1937 season should have been a good one for the people in the town connected with the holiday trade. In addition to the special lights the town was also host to a major international roller hockey festival.

THE HORSE-DRAWN BRAKES of the early years of the century (see p. 28 top) were replaced in the age of motors by the sort of vehicle seen here parked outside the pier theatre. The French name *char à banc* originally referred to a carriage with benches and this became generally applied to any vehicle with rows of transverse seats. This group could be the pier staff off on their annual outing in October 1926. At the back the second figure in from the right is Dick Wild who worked at the rink, and in the front row third in from the left is Percy Carey the entertainments manager.

Entertainment and Sport

*Football – Walking – Angling – Rowing – Roller Hockey – Bands
Concert Parties – Amateur Societies*

HERNE BAY FOOTBALL TEAM SEASON 1890–91. The team left to right standing are: C.H. Fox, J. Welby, F. Sherwood, A. Hogbin, A. Freer; middle row on chairs: C.A. Lumley (goal keeper), T.F. Ridout, E.L. Mobbs, A.S. Walker; sitting on the ground: H. Boulding (left) and P.G. Admans (right). G. Simms and R. Greaves also played that season. Between December 1890 and April 1891 Herne Bay played against Faversham, New Court, Whitstable, Sittingbourne, Kent College and Kent Coast College. Charlie Fox went on to play for Tottenham Hotspur in 1905/6. Fox was the licensee of the Victoria in the High Street, and is remembered as one of the 'fathers' of roller hockey in the town. He continued refereeing for years after he finished playing and can be seen in the picture at the top of p. 122.

WALKING RACES WERE A POPULAR PART of the local scene in the early 1900s. The best remembered sponsor of such events was William Godden of Little Smithfield in the High Street. Godden was a strong believer in the power of advertising and found any number of ways to get his name noticed by the public. This picture shows a walking race on the track around the Cycle and Athletic Ground in 1905 (now William street car park). The fence on the left runs along the top of the bank at the back of the pavement to Beach Street.

THIS PICTURE SHOWS THE LADIES' RACE on the same day. The contestants' outfits look somewhat restrictive by today's standards. The large sloping roof seen centrally in the background belongs to Mitchell's Cycle Hall. This building was used for all sorts of entertainments and Mitchell himself sponsored various cycle and foot races. To the right behind the Union Jack we can see the backs of what are now Nos 118, 120 and 122 High Street. To their right there is a boarded fence showing an undeveloped gap where the library now stands. The row of houses running off the picture to the right are actually on the north side of the High Street. The first one can be clearly seen as Eastwell House, the present home of the Constitutional Club.

THE BEST KNOWN LOCAL WALKING MATCH was Godden's Derby. There were various races on the appointed day including a ladies' handicap and men's six mile handicap. The main event was over eleven and a half miles and involved four laps of a course that started in the High Street, then down to Sea Street, over Station Bridge into Eddington Lane, on to Canterbury Road and back to the High Street. The event took its name from William Godden a local butcher and sportsman with a considerable flair for publicity. At the evening smoking concerts which followed the races Godden invariably complained that the event should be known as the Herne Bay Derby. In 1906 Godden put up a Challenge Cup for the event. This photograph shows W. Rose who won the cup outright in 1910, having also won for the previous two years. At the presentation in the Pier Theatre Rose also received a gold medal, a signet ring and a purse. In 1910 the event was covered by the *Daily Mirror*.

THIS PHOTOGRAPH SHOWS WALKERS passing Parr's Bank (now the National Westminster Bank) and Charles Cole's the hairdressers. Godden's shop, Little Smithfield, is just out of the photograph to the right. The men pacing on bicycles were sometimes in difficulties when the crowds began to close in towards the end of a race. The format of four laps around the town must have maximized the interest for the spectators. When Rose won the Cup in 1910 his time for eleven and a half miles was one hour fifty minutes. This race was extremely popular, and many years later in the 1930s it was adopted by the local paper who used the event to raise funds for the local hospital. A similar event was tried in the 1960s over a course that included the seafront.

THIS PICTURE TAKEN FURTHER DOWN THE HIGH STREET may have been taken on the same day. The large gap in the buildings on the right is now filled by the library. Nimrod Samuel Mitchell, owner of the Cycle Hall and adjacent shop, was one of the committee that not only helped Godden with this event but also organized other sporting events on the grounds to the rear of his premises. The left-hand side of Mitchell's property is now a mini-market.

THE TOPE *GALEORHINUS GALEUS* is a member of the same shark family as the blue shark and the man-eating tiger shark. The tope enters shallow coastal waters in the summer months and in the early 1900s large numbers were caught at Herne Bay, providing sport fishing that attracted anglers from far and wide. Each season the first catches of 'dogs' were reported in the London newspapers. This photograph taken just east of the pier shows a proud captor with a couple of good fish. The badge on his straw hat is probably that of the Heron Angling Association. The boats in the picture are typical of those used in the early years of this sport fishing, when tope up to six feet in length were caught within a mile or two of the beach. In 1912 at their annual dinner the Herne Bay Angling Association reported a total weight of tope landed for the season of 2,000 lb. By the 1920s motor boats were needed to search further afield for increasingly elusive fish. An awareness of the finite nature of fish stocks means that today most tope caught on rod and line are returned to the sea alive.

IN 1932 THE HERNE BAY ANGLING ASSOCIATION fished its annual tope festival over two days in early June. On Saturday eighteen competitors landed twelve fish, on Sunday twenty-two competitors landed twelve fish. This photograph shows both days' catch. Reading from the left the large boatman leaning on the winch is the unmistakable bulk of Bill Blogg, behind him is Frank Holness (father of Ernie), below Bill on the shingle is Jesse Mount, next to him is Puddeny Pressley (Ninetie's brother), the lady on the left is Mrs Plante, next Mrs Gay and then Mrs Stableford. The young man standing on the right is Bert Harrington, scout leader and fishing tackle dealer. Among the visitors at the railings are Mr Percy Cooper, fifth from the left with beret, pipe and bow tie. Ninth from the left with the cap and moustache is Mr Osman (this is the man that gave his name to the first bay on the pier, his favourite fishing spot). Thirteenth from the left with the neat rounded collar is another fishing tackle dealer Mr Patterson and next to him with the bow tie and neat white beard is Mr Stableford. Mrs Plante won the competition with a top weight of 94 lb 1 oz. The total weight for the twenty-four fish was 723 lbs 11 oz. Mrs Plante, a formidable angler, won this competition in 1926, 1932, 1933 and 1935. Mrs Gay won in 1927 and 1934.

THESE TWO ANGLERS ARE FISHING FROM THE NECK of the pier below the tent prior to the widening in 1910 (see p. 58). This looks more relaxing than catching tope. Admission to the pier was 1d, with a fishing ticket another 1d (less than 1p total).

THE HERNE BAY ANGLING ASSOCIATION'S most prestigious trophy is this solid silver Championship Shield decorated with views of the town and angling devices. It was first competed for in 1906. In 1907 it was won by Mr W.H. Begbie, of the Hastings and St Leonards club. This picture shows the shield on display at Hastings. It is still competed for at the annual boat festival.

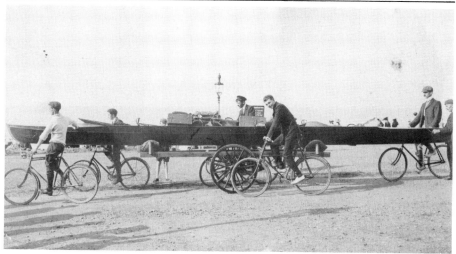

IN THE PAST THIS PHOTOGRAPH HAS ERRONEOUSLY BEEN CAPTIONED 'How they got to the Regatta'. From the club's earliest days in the 1880s regattas were attended all round the south coast. Unlike today these events were held mid-week, usually on a town's early closing day and it was not unusual for three regattas to be rowed in a week. These pictures date from 1904; I am sure that they in fact show no more than how the boats were transported to and from the various railway stations. In later years open lorries were used, sometimes with the crews huddled in the back. When funds and support ran to it, coaches were used with the boats on the roof.

PHOTO, BY
J. PEMBERTON,
HERNE BAY.

THERE HAVE BEEN A NUMBER OF GOLDEN PERIODS in the club's history when the Herne Bay Amateur Rowing Club have swept through all the opposition. One of the names to emerge in the early years was Gipson. Brothers Bert and Cecil raced in single sculls, pairs and fours. Many trophies were won outright and for years these would be seen in the old library museum. Bert probably had the better record on the coast. In 1909 at the age of twenty-five Cecil gave up his amateur status to row professionally. A series of matches was held on the Thames and out of forty-five competitors Cecil went through a week's heats to eventually beat Ernest Barry the Champion of England. The winner's purse was forty-five pounds.

MILITARY SPORTS AND GYMKHANA. Through the years of the First World War various events were organized around the town to raise funds for the welfare of the troops. In 1917 the organizer's committee under Brigadier General the Hon. W.E. Cavendish MVO announced that there would be military sports and a gymkhana and the event was to be held on the sports ground that is now William Street car park. The massed bands of the Hampshire and Devonshire Regiments were to play in the afternoon. There were more than thirty events with the emphasis on fun and hundreds of people turned up to watch. The list of regiments taking part included Somerset, Devon, Hants, Australian Infantry, Rifle Brigade, RAMC and the South Staffordshire Regiment. The novelty races included a wheelbarrow race (with the driver blindfolded), potato race, sack race and race in gas helmets. This photograph shows the Officers' animal race. The man with the pig is 2nd Lieut. Armstrong who came second. I regret to say the two chickens and the goat were unplaced and the winner was a Lieut. Sapcote with a monkey. Perhaps he had already crossed the line when this photograph was taken.

DURING THE FIRST WORLD WAR the local football leagues were badly hit by the disappearance of so many able-bodied young men who were away serving their King. What the area did have in abundance was troops camped locally before moving on to the Continent. Matches between army sides were popular, with locals turning out to encourage the players. This picture taken by Palmer shows an East Kent Yeomanry team. At this time the area bounded by Station Road, Western Avenue, Sea Street and Fleetwood Avenue was largely un-developed and was home to thousands of men living under canvas. St George's Public Hall (now a car showroom in Sea Street just north of York Road) was used as a mess facility and for a number of troop entertainments.

HARRY BEDWELL seen here in 1934 at the side of the Pier Pavilion. Harry played for Herne Bay Juniors in 1927, for Herne Bay Roller Hockey and Skating Club 1st team in 1931, and was club captain between 1932 and 1953. He played for England at Lisbon in 1947. During this period the club were twice champions of Great Britain. He retired as a player in 1953 but carried on refereeing. He was Hon. Secretary in 1957 and Chairman in 1960. Sid Bedwell, Harry's younger brother also played for the club. Harry was described in the sporting press at the time of his retirement as 'Unassuming and a sportsman of the finest calibre ... '.

HOCKEY CLUB FRESNOY OF FRANCE met the Herne Bay Rink Hockey Club in their third and deciding encounter on the 4 January 1922. Herne Bay first played and beat Fresnoy in 1921, and the return at Roubaix went to the French side. The Herne Bay team for the decider were, left to right: Budge, Freddie Barling, Ernie Maybourne, R. Hoile, George Fox. Fox scored in the first half but the game went to Fresnoy 1–3. Standing to the left of the picture is Mr G. Cursons (President, Herne Bay Roller Hockey & Skating Club), standing on the right is Charlie Fox (referee), kneeling in front of him is D. Spence-Whyte (Hon. general secretary HBRH & SC). Maybourne (in goal) took over the captaincy for this match as the club captain Jack Derham did not play. The photograph taken by Percy Hargreaves is at the north end of the old pier pavilion rink.

THE 8TH EUROPEAN RINK HOCKEY CHAMPIONSHIP was played at the Pier Pavilion in May 1934. This photograph taken in the Central Bandstand shows the six teams that took part. The England team with four Herne Bay players won all five games. The team pictured are, left to right: R. Hulme (Derby Flyers), P. Walters (Herne Bay), E. Bowa (Herne Bay), C. Williams (Ilford), W. Sutton (All Blacks London), G. Spice (Herne Bay), P. Monk (ex Faversham) and the team goal-keeper was F. Payton (Herne Bay). The keeper in the photograph, C. Williams, was a reserve, as were Spice and Monk. On finals night an England side beat the rest 4–3. Spice, Monk and Williams all played in this side and George Spice scored the winning goal. The total attendance for the four nights matches at the pier pavilion was 6,118.

HERNE BAY.

WEEKLY PROGRAMME OF

ENTERTAINMENTS

UNDER THE DIRECTION OF THE URBAN DISTRICT COUNCIL.

ARTHUR J. BARCLAY - - - Entertainments Manager.

On MONDAY, AUGUST 22nd & during the week

BAND OF H.M.

ROYAL GARRISON ARTILLERY

Under the Direction of Mr. P. F. BATTISHILL

WILL PLAY:-

THE DOWNS, 11 to 12.30.　　　TOWER GARDENS, 3 to 5.

IF WET IN THE NEW PAVILION ON PIER.　(Chair Tickets available).

THE PIER - 8 to 10.

SUNDAY ON THE PIER 3 to 5 & 7 to 9 o'clock

VOCALISTS:

MISS NORA ALEXANDER

AND MR.

LAWRENCE CRESFIELD

AUGUST 22nd, 23rd & 24th,	AUGUST 25th, 26th & 27th,
"FLORODORA"	Miss GLOSSOP-HARRIS'
Mr. CHARLES CONSTANT'S CO.	SHAKESPEAREAN COMPANY.

Will appear in the PIER PAVILION THEATRE at 8 o'clock.

DOORS OPEN 7.30

IN THE AFTERNOON OF WEDNESDAY, AUG. 24th, A

FANCY & PRIVATE DRESS JUVENILE BALL

IN GRAND PAVILION FROM 3 TO 5.30.　VALUABLE PRIZES & SOUVENIRS GIVEN.

THE JOLLITY BOYS

Perform Daily at the Al Fresco Theatre on the Downs, 12.30 to 1.30, at 3.30 in the Afternoon, & every Evening at 8

Daily change of Programme

In case of wet or Inclement weather, the Jollity Boys will perform in the East Cliff Pavilion.
Afternoon and Evening in the Town Hall, as occasion may require.

THIS POSTER FOR HERNE BAY ENTERTAINMENTS was produced in 1910 by Frank Ridout. There are more than a dozen different type faces in use on this one poster and the setting, in wooden type, would have taken about three and a half hours. Frank's son Jack remembers that as a boy he collected the next week's programme from the band sergeants. This information was updated as new posters were produced for each week of the season. This family-run print business is now in its fourth generation; it was established in 1855 by Frank's father.

THE MILITARY BANDS were hugely popular and in August 1905 more than 800 people attended one evening concert in the marquee on the pier. Apart from their performances at the various regular bandstands it was not unknown for bands to attend private functions at Strode Park and elsewhere. Special arrangements were also made for all-day events such as the Regattas. The conductors were minor local celebrities and this photograph shows one such officer standing in front of the bandstand on top of the King's Hall.

FOR MANY VISITORS a doze in a chair breathing in the fresh sea breezes while listening to a military band was an essential ingredient of a day at the seaside. This picture shows the Band of the Royal Engineers playing at the flagstaff in August 1905. Originally the bands were engaged by the Herne Bay Military Band Committee and this group recovered their costs by letting out chairs for the listeners and by holding fund raising events out of season. The committee was dissolved in December 1909 when the Herne Bay Urban District Council took over their role.

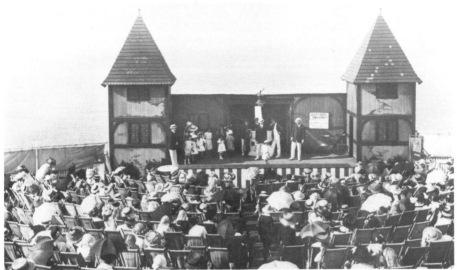

THE AUTHORITIES SEEM TO HAVE TAKEN A PRAGMATIC VIEW of how to deal with the various artists wishing to perform at Herne Bay in the early 1900s. In April 1902 nine groups made application for the three 'official' sites. In that year the Herne Bay Minstrels held on to their Clock Tower pitch (see p. 37) and the Jollity Boys retained the East Cliff. In 1904 the Jollity Boys held on to the East Cliff site, despite not putting in the highest bid and applying outside of the correct time span. With their feet thus firmly under the table the Jollity Boys developed this pitch with the Fun Towers that can be seen in this picture. The HBBC on the chairs seems to indicate that they were making use of chairs belonging to the Herne Bay Band Committee.

THE EAST CLIFF ENTERTAINERS had always benefited from customers being able to take advantage of the natural rake of the grassy slopes. As the fun towers stage was developed so the seating area was enclosed and a more formal arrangement for seating developed. In this picture the seats are empty because the band is playing; performances were carefully timed so as not to clash. Beyond the band a line of customers can be seen patiently waiting on the jetty below the Clock Tower. This jetty was used by the beach boats as the tide fell away, extending the length of time when they were able to offer trips round the bay.

CONCERT PARTIES were a hugely popular form of entertainment. This picture shows the line up of the Jollity Boys for 1910. Towards the end of each season benefit concerts were held for particular artists. The figure second from the right is Charles Howard and his benefit night was 20 August. The review in the local paper tells us that every seat in the enclosure was taken (see previous page) and that four to five thousand stood outside the fence. To maximize the gate at these benefits performers from other groups appearing in the town would do special guest spots.

RONALD CECIL appeared at Herne Bay with his concert party in 1912. In July that year they were billed to perform at the stage by the flagstaff in the Tower Gardens and in the Grand Pavilion if wet. This photograph shows Mr James Henry on the left and Ronald Cecil on the right; the two ladies are Miss Lily Austin and Miss Hilda Gerald-Poel.

IN 1905 THE GAIETY BOYS somehow managed to secure the East Cliff stage, ousting the Jollity Boys. John Forge had been bringing this troupe to the town since 1902. In this publicity photograph are George Greystone, John Forge, Albert Chapman, Charles Douglas, Ernest Cutting, Alfred Fishey and Harvey Warwick. Within particular troupes artists would change from season to season, some performers only spending part of the summer at the seaside, returning the rest of the time to the music halls.

THE GAIETY BOYS WERE BACK ON THE WEST CLIFF in 1906. This pitch on the beach midway between the pier and Lane End was the least popular with the performers. Being west of the pier it was not on a route to anywhere and the position right on the beach also meant that it was liable to damage in a good north-west blow. In 1902 when the annual charge for the East Cliff stage was ten pounds, this pitch was only five pounds for the season. John Forge's own benefit in September 1906 was a victim of the weather and was held in the Town Hall.

Mʳ Fred Wilson.

ROUSE, WAY AND WILSON were not only the longest lasting concert party to perform at Herne Bay but they were probably also the most commercially minded. As early as 1902 they were holding alfresco concerts at their own ground in Avenue Road. Virtually every visitor to the town that arrived by train would pass this site. With their own site they also avoided the lottery of bidding for the recognized pitches on the front. This publicity photograph of Fred Wilson interestingly shows a backcloth that may depict the East Cliff Pavilion. In 1913 at the council meeting where the successful contractor's tender for the new King's Hall was accepted, the trio offered to underwrite the venture with a payment of £700 per year for seven years. This proposal was effectively scuttled by the outbreak of war the following year.

Opposite:

RILEY'S REVELLERS. The advertising in the local paper for August 1912 describes this troupe in the following glowing terms: 'Under the auspices of the Herne Bay Urban District Council. Mr R.J. Garfield Dutton presents Riley's Revellers, a merry party of juveniles in a mirthful medley of fun and frolic.' Although they were billed as unique they were appearing on the West Cliff which was not the most favoured pitch.

WILLIE ROUSE seated at the same dressing table as his partner Way in Fred Palmer's studio opposite the Clock Tower. Rouse and Wilson continued to work together after the death of Way. Their premises in Avenue Road were used by the YMCA through the war years and soon after 1918 they changed the name to Bohemia. In 1924 Willie Rouse broadcast on the stage of the Bohemia from the British Broadcasting Station 2LO London. The broadcast was about the history of the music halls. In 1926 'Wireless Willie' as he was known was broadcasting with his son Wilfred. Willie died in 1928 and the premises were leased by Mr W. Broadbent who continued the business under the name Gaiety until the premises were destroyed by fire in 1932.

HOWELL TAGGART WAY preferred to be known on stage as Owen. In the trio's early years at Herne Bay Mrs Way would often perform with them. In 1908 they further developed the site in Avenue Road with a purpose-built hall. As well as entertaining visitors through the season they did special performances for a variety of local charities. In 1912 they even put on a Christmas special. Owen Way died at the age of fifty-five in 1919.

JESSIE FILER'S LADIES ORCHESTRA seen here on the stage of the New Central Bandstand. In August 1928 the orchestra was sharing the evening bill at the Pier Pavilion. For 1s 6d (7½p) music fans could listen to the ladies along with the Balalaika Orchestra plus Valerie Port and her twin sister. Other entertainers playing at Herne Bay that August included the bands of the 2nd Battalion of the Buffs and the Argyll & Sutherland Highlanders. The timing of the various performances was such that a stroll from the East Cliff to the Pier could include at least three programmes of music.

KITCHEN SYMPHONY: what are they doing and why? Your guess is as good as mine. The picture dates from the early 1900s. The columns are supporting the upper deck of the East Cliff Pavilion. The rather formal clothes of the period tend to make the young ladies look older than they may really be. In 1905 there were at least six ladies' schools no further away than Downs Park and Sea View Road. Whatever the event they all look remarkably serious.

HERNE BAY AMATEUR OPERATIC SOCIETY, 1908. From the earliest days of the town Herne Bay has been able to boast a number of strong amateur theatrical groups. The *Herne Bay Press* of 1884 mentions the preliminary meeting of the Amateur Dramatic Club at the Brunswick Hotel. This picture shows the cast of the *Mikado* rather squashed into Mr Palmer's studio. The performance at the Town Hall in the High Street was booked for Tuesday 28 and Wednesday 29 April. Support was in fact so good that there was a further performance on the Thursday. The cast list reads rather like a trade directory for the High Street businesses. The Howell family between them cover Chee-Ki (the boy in the centre), Peep-Bo, Yum Yum and a member of the chorus. Even the school's headmaster Mr Flower is among the Nobles, Guards and Coolies somewhere.

THE BELLE OF NEW YORK 1921. The Herne Bay Bohemians Operatic and Dramatic Society had a hit on their hands with this production at the Pier Theatre. Originally booked for the 7, 8, 9 and 10 December the management were pleased to announce that the heavy demand for seating would allow an extra performance on the following Monday. Among the business advertisements in the programme the competition for live theatre makes an appearance. Jackie Coogan 'The Kid' (himself) was at the Casino Cinema and Pearl White was in the 'Tigers Cub' at the Bijou in the High Street.

LES CLOCHES DE CORNEVILLE. In May 1924 this production was credited to the Operatic Society. The comic opera was reported in the local paper as a great success. This photograph of the cast was taken just in front of the columned entrance to the Pier Pavilion. The two small boys in the front (they were pages) are Phil and Tubby Roma.

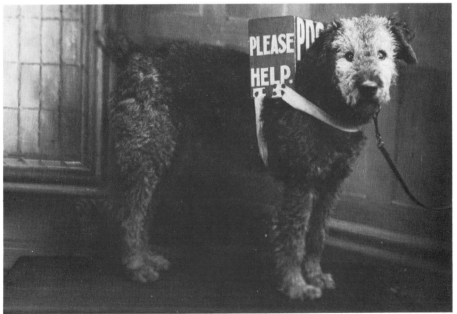

NO COLLECTION OF LOCAL PHOTOGRAPHS WOULD BE COMPLETE without a dog portrait. At the town Dog and Cat Show in August 1928 Gunner, owned by Mrs Cakebread, was presented with a medal in recognition of his support for the PDSA. Tragically, Gunner was fatally struck by a car on Beacon Hill in 1930. Articles about the dog and his work featured on the front page of the local newspaper for no less than three weeks.

PIER DIVERS AND EXHIBITION SWIMMERS were a popular form of entertainment at the seaside. Some of the early performers seem to favour the title 'Professor'; one such was a Professor Powsey who visited the town in the 1890s. In 1938 Miss Gladys Powsey, trick swimmer and diver, was giving exhibitions at the pier head at 11.30 a.m. and 3.30 p.m. This lady had been featured at the Women's Fair at Olympia in the same year. The same name may be a coincidence or the two performers may have been related; either way Miss Powsey eventually retired to the area and lived at Broomfield.

Around and About

*Herne – Beltinge – Broomfield – Reculver – Hampton – Schools
Camps – Scouts – Military*

THE MAIN ROAD BETWEEN HERNE BAY AND CANTERBURY. This picture clearly illustrates the totally different pace of village life possible when the fastest traffic was horse-drawn. Emma Dilnot stands in front of the post office where today cars, lorries and buses rush by. In 1900 it was difficult to miss the name Dilnot in Herne. John Dilnot was the post-master, grocer, baker and draper; Frank Dilnot was the village butcher; Harry Dilnot was the assistant overseer and Clerk to the Parish Council; Thomas Dilnot was the Registrar of Births and Deaths. The advertising brochures for Herne Bay invariably describe the pleasures of walks through the well-wooded countryside south of the town. Herne had a variety of attractions and the ancient parish church of St Martin's was famous for its brasses and architecture. At a more practical level the Lower Red Lion was noted for its tea gardens. It may seem strange now but in the early 1960s when the projecting buildings on the far right were demolished there was a considerable body of opinion that also wanted to demolish the smugglers' cottages (in the right foreground). The local newspaper reported that 'As Herne Bay and Whitstable were developing Herne did not want to be left behind when it came to modernisation'.

THE VIEW UP SCHOOL LANE from the gate of Herne church has not changed a great deal in eighty years. On the left the windows of the smugglers' cottages were changed considerably during rebuilding. The Prince Albert has become The Smugglers with Shepherd Neame in place of George Beer and Rigdens Ales. The village butcher is still established on the corner but unlike Frank Dilnot he is no longer an agent for Jones sewing machines nor does he have a wicket gate to keep dogs out of the shop. The cottage to the right has lost its patriotic flag but gained an unfortunate 'Georgian' bay window. 'Sunnyside' on the right has managed to survive in a remarkably original state.

RECULVER ROAD around 1910. Many visitors to Herne Bay passed through Beltinge *en route* to Reculver. Fred Port ran his carriage business from the garage in the centre and apart from the source of motor power the business is much the same today. The land and buildings beyond have been redeveloped up to Hazlemere Drive. The large building with the black and white gables was then the Beltinge Supply Stores Co. Ltd managed by Alec Luck. From the 1920s Beltinge has grown quickly with more and more houses being developed to either side of Reculver Road. Despite all the new building this part of Beltinge has somehow managed to retain some sort of village character.

BROOMFIELD VILLAGE POND dried out in June 1921. There was general agreement that this provided a splendid opportunity for it to be cleaned out. This photograph taken by Scrivens in July shows exactly what was involved when the only horse power available was pulling the carts. This job must have kept these men employed for quite a few weeks. The hand pump being used, although no doubt serviceable, was something of an antique in 1921.

FEBRUARY 1929 WAS A PARTICULARLY COLD MONTH (see p. 17 bottom). E.J. Simmons of Minster Drive took this photograph showing people skating on the frozen pond at Broomfield. In the background there are even people playing hockey. As well as this pond skaters also used the frozen dykes at Reculver.

RECULVER, SOME FOUR MILES EAST OF HERNE BAY, has long been a popular spot with visitors. The remains of the Roman fort and the early church provide a good excuse for a walk along the cliffs. In the late 1880s the proprietor of the Tower Hotel, J. Collard, not only ran horse-drawn brakes to the Towers but he also sponsored regattas there as an added attraction and provided the catering for the visitors while they waited for his vehicles to take them home. This picture was taken in the mid-1920s. The skeletal vanes on the towers replace lead covered spires and the vegetables in the foreground are growing inside the walls of the Roman fort. The house and cottages, some of which served teas to visitors, were demolished in the 1960s.

RECULVER'S TWIN TOWERS are sometimes known as the sisters. In October 1923 the south tower was struck by lightning. The local newspaper tells us that the fire was put out by the Herne Bay brigade under Lieut C.W. Welby (one witness has told me that the fire had burnt itself out before they got there). The row of houses on the skyline are the coastguard cottages. Demolished while still basically sound, their removal has left open a part of the Roman fort that has yet to receive a comprehensive archaeological dig. This photograph taken from a point due south of the Ethelbert provides a reminder of how rural the spot once was.

HAMPTON-ON-SEA seen from the foot of Hampton Hill. The outer row of houses are the seaward end of Hernecliff Gardens. At auction in 1888 plots in this road were averaging thirteen pounds each. The inner shorter row is in Eddington Gardens; in the same auction plots in this road made only eight to nine pounds each. The sales were held in the summer and most of the purchasers came down from London for the day. Nine years later the great storm of 1897 (see p. 10) sent waves right through some of the houses in Hernecliff Gardens and in July 1899 the end house was undermined by the sea. In this picture piles of materials can be seen where a house has been demolished on the seaward end of the row.

A STORMY DAY. This picture shows the low ground between the brook and the houses during a stiff onshore blow. In September 1905 the Land Company of Cheapside tried to sell (leasehold) eleven brick-built slate-roofed cottage villas at Hampton known as 1–12 Hernecliff Gardens. Bids ranged from forty to eighty pounds and only one was sold, the rest being bought in for the vendor. In the same sale forty-five pounds would buy a freehold plot in Albany or Minster Drive.

HERNECLIFF GARDENS SEEN FROM STUDD HILL. This view shows the grave difficulties faced by the people living in these houses. When the engineers of the Herne Bay, Hampton and Reculver Oyster Fishery Co. built the pier in the 1860s they had not appreciated the problems it would cause. Beach built up on the east side but to the west the pier set up a scour which rapidly eroded the unprotected soft clay cliffs. The area between the front of the houses and Hampton Hill where the brook ran out to the sea was very low-lying. When a high spring tide coincided with an onshore wind and a period of prolonged rainfall these houses were practically surrounded by water.

HAMPTON HILL WITH ITS SPLENDID VIEWS towards the Swale and easy access to the beach had long been a popular camping site. This picture was taken looking up the hill from what is now Hampton Pier Avenue. The two houses are Nos. 5 and 7 West Cliff Gardens. Although the camp has an efficient military look to it the campers may still be youth groups. Many such groups came down from London and elsewhere to stay at camps laid out by ex-military personnel using equipment hired for the season. As late as 1922 the *Herne Bay Press* lists sixteen different youth camps in the area, seven of which were at Hampton.

THE MAN WITH THE WHITE BEARD was Edmund Reid. This character lived in the end house of Eddington Gardens, No. 4 Eddington Villas, or 'Reid's Ranch' as it was known. The hut in this photograph was at the end of the garden. From here Reid sold lemonade and postcards illustrating disappearing Hampton. Reid had been born in Canterbury but worked as a lad in London. He joined the police in 1872 and at 5 ft 6½ in he was the shortest man in the force. He was appointed a detective and worked within what was to become the CID at Bethnal Green. A move to Whitechapel meant that he worked on the infamous 'Ripper' murders. In twenty-three years' service he received fifty-three commendations. On top of all that he held the Gold and Bronze medals of the Balloon Society of Great Britain, making twenty-three ascents from Crystal Palace and Alexandra Palace. He moved to Eddington Villas in 1903 from an address in the town and in 1898 he was the licensee of the Lower Red Lion at Herne.

VISITING SCOUT TROOPS were probably delighted to have their photograph taken with this slightly eccentric gent. Reid had battlements and cannons painted on the end wall of his house to deter any would-be invaders.

THE *HERNE BAY PRESS* in March 1910 carried a letter from Reid claiming that he and two others had built a bridge over the brook. This work, which they considered essential to save a long detour, took three days and he submitted a bill to the council for three pounds. This picture shows the culvert that caused so many problems and what may be Reid's own bridge. In April another letter appeared; the council had returned Reid's bill but the Board of Trade (to whom Reid had written direct) had instructed the council to clear the obstruction. With donations from his neighbours coming to £1 0s 6d Reid concluded that bridge building was not a paying concern.

THE NOVELTY OF THESE HOUSES and their predicament was something of an attraction to visitors. This situation was to be exploited by Reid seen here standing on the remains of an early sea defence. The large sections of pipe behind him were not for drainage but were a part of the wall and at low tide large pieces of such pipe can still be found all over this area. As the land owner was involved in property and development on a large scale elsewhere, it is possible they were surplus from another project.

THIS END PROPERTY would seem to be the one that has been reduced to piles of rubble in the picture at the top of p. 140. Once again Reid manages to get himself in the picture.

THIS VIEW LOOKING DOWN FROM HAMPTON HILL can be compared with the picture p. 140 top. Hernecliff Gardens are a thing of the past; the sea-washed clay at the end of Reid's garden shows where an average high tide was reaching. Some trace of the ponds that were to be used as boating lakes can be seen in front of and between the old cottage and Eddington Villas.

APART FROM THE PHOTOGRAPHS THAT REID HAS LEFT showing us what Hampton was like he also wrote a stream of amusing letters to the local newspaper. His dry humour was usually aimed at the apparent deficiencies in the work of the authorities particularly as they affected his empire. The mouth of Hampton brook flowed to the sea via a culvert through the shingle and this culvert was often blocked causing the water and weed to back up and stagnate. In correspondence Reid would refer to this as 'the lavender brook'.

THIS VIEW OF HAMPTON shows the scene with only Eddington Villas and the old cottage left. The isolated rock in the water (which can still be seen today at low water) is the very western most end of the curved sea wall across the end of Hernecliff Gardens (this can be seen in detail at the Bottom of p. 143). The last two houses of Eddington Villas were bought for demolition by local builder Edgar Edwards and the salvaged materials were used to construct a bungalow which still stands in the Broadway. The town is spreading west and the green fields of Hampton Hill are disappearing.

AND THEN THERE WERE NONE. All that remains to show the presence of any houses is the ring of rocks of the old sea defences. The old farmhouse can just be made out to the right on the very edge of the high water mark. More buildings have appeared on the hill and the Hampton Inn now stands on an island site. This road improvement was carried out to ease the corner for the increasing number of motor cars that were visiting the town.

IN THE EARLY 1930s the land owner at Hampton, Mr Ramuz, decided to make something out of what remained of his rather wet site. One of the old oyster breeding ponds was enlarged to provide a boating lake. The boats to be used were electric and came from the Glida Boat Co. of Canvey Island. One of the men who built the boats in Essex was Harry Chalk who came to Herne Bay to run the business. Harry found himself spending the first winter enlarging the ponds and using the excavated material to form some sort of sea defence. This photograph shows the level of the ponds relative to the beach beyond. The isolated rock in the sea can also be seen in the picture opposite.

THE LEISURE VENTURE AT HAMPTON was successful. The electric Glida boats were moved round to the concrete pools to the west of the pier and new boats with petrol engines were used at Hampton. In this photograph Hampton Hill is still relatively undeveloped. The motor boat pond is almost in its final form with the central island dug out. With changes in public demand and the dead hand of the local authority on the tiller this facility declined rapidly after Harry retired in 1966.

HERNE BAY COUNCIL SCHOOL BOYS. The date on the slate is 1904 and the man on the left is W.J. Flower the headmaster. The career of this gentleman included the earliest years of organized schooling in the town. He started work in the William Street Boys' School on 13 June 1870, which was in the small building south of the parish church built by the generosity of Mrs Ann Thwaites in 1839. He was the only teacher with fifty-two scholars. In 1880 there was an amalgamation of boys and girls assembled in the Mortimer Street building under a joint committee of church and non-conformist managers. Mr Flower was then headmaster with some 350 children. In 1881 the jurisdiction of the committee changed and the school came under Herne School Board. Eventually the New Board School opened in Kings Road on 25 June 1887 (the new schools were described as being 'situated in open fields at the back of the town') and Mr Flower was headmaster, with his wife in charge of the girls. They both retired on 31 January 1912. Mr Flowers had had forty-two years of service, his wife thirty-five years. He died on 14 March 1919 aged seventy-two. Apart from his job as headmaster he sat on any number of local boards and committees.

THE VILLAGE SCHOOLS around Herne Bay had to work on a different scale to the town schools. As late as 1915 the average roll at Reculver School was never above fifty. This photograph taken in the early 1900s not only shows a good average attendance but both members of staff as well.

THE MAYPOLE. This picture was taken by Pemberton at one of Herne Bay's many private schools in about 1903. The serious part of the day would appear to be the presentation of certificates with the dancing as an entertainment for visitors and friends. In about 1910 when the fees at Belle Vue on the seafront were twenty guineas per term, dancing was an extra at one and a half guineas.

SEVERAL PEOPLE WHO HAVE SEEN THIS PHOTOGRAPH remember the man on the right not as A.A. Hodgkison BA, headmaster of King's Road Council School (boys), but as Buggins. After more than fifty years no one has given me an explanation of the origin of the head's nickname. The event shown may be a school fête or perhaps it is one of the many fund raising fairs organized by the Cheerful Sparrows on the site of what is now William Street car park.

KINGS ROAD SCHOOL. It is quite likely that some of the children in this photograph and the photograph top right appear elsewhere in this book. The school originally opened in 1887 and had to expand to accommodate the growth in the town's population. The teacher on the right at the back is Miss Curling. She is remembered as something of a disciplinarian although as several now elderly ladies have said to me it hasn't done them any harm.

A BOYS' CLASS photographed at around the same time. Today there would be howls of protest at the idea of the girls all sitting with a piece of sewing on their desks while the boys are shown with books and pencils.

MORE MAYPOLE DANCERS, although this group somehow do not look quite so well turned out as the girls on p. 149. The photograph was taken by Palmer and the girls are standing in front of the cricket pavilion in the corner of the playing field behind Kent Coast College. This private boys' school stood in Canterbury Road (now No. 23 and divided into flats) and their sports field stretched up Beltinge Hill towards Beacon Road. A part of these grounds is still used for sport by the Herne Bay Hockey and Lawn Tennis Club. It would be interesting to hear what an Edwardian groundsman might have to say about the artificial turf that covers the pitch at Kent Close today.

MAY DAY 1921 was a big day for Miss Cissie Hill; she was crowned a May Queen at the Infants' School in King's Road. Most of the maids of honour look happy enough but the boy with the bugle looks apprehensive in his role as herald.

BOYS' BRIGADE CAMP. This photograph shows one of the many youth groups that came to camp at Herne Bay. The bank in the background is probably the railway embankment. The boys' brigade often used a site off Canterbury Road north of the railway line where a block of sheltered flats now stands. The man fourth from the left in the second row from the front is Harold Smith. In the late 1930s Smith retired to Herne Bay and lived with his mother at Maybush in Canterbury Road. In retirement he continued his work with the 1st Herne Bay Company Boys' Brigade.

THE 1ST HERNE BAY BOY SCOUT TROOP can claim to be one of the first in the country. This troop was a development of a Boys' Guild (founded in 1906) and ran in connection with the Congregational church by Mr Norman Miller. The appeal of Baden Powell's ideas was such that at least sixty-four troops across the country claim to have been formed in 1908 (the first issue of Baden Powell's *Scouting for Boys* went on sale in January 1908). Norman Miller's Tiger, Peacock, Lion and Eagle patrols certainly have good claim to be among the 'first'. These two pictures each show an area known latterly as St Anne's Playing Field, now occupied by blocks of flats. The buildings on the right are the backs of the row of shops and houses where Station Road meets the High Street. The large rendered building stood in the High Street on the site of St Anne's filling station. Some of Herne Bay's first Boy Scouts appear elsewhere in this book: Billy Smeed (p. 79 top) and Harry Bedwell (p. 121 bottom) lived long enough to enjoy a Jubilee reunion in 1957 with their leader Bert Harrington (seen as a young man on p. 117). The pictures on p. 106 show scouts of the 1st Herne Bay performing ceremonial duties at the Town Hall War Memorial.

B COMPANY KENT CYCLISTS found themselves stationed at Herne in October 1914 and this picture shows a group relaxing at the pier head. Although the bicycles are not identical each have the straps that were used to hold the men's rifles in place. We know some of their names: at the back on the right is cyclist C.N. Jupp, sitting on the right is cyclist A. Allenshaw, and two of the other four at the back are C. Russell and J.E. Holland.

LEWIS GUN PRACTICE. This group of soldiers attended a Lewis gun course at Herne Bay in the early years of the First World War. They are on what was then a sports ground, now William Street car park, and in the background behind the fence is the parish church and south school room. An inquisitive child peeps through a gap in the fence. From left to right the regiments represented are: Hampshire Regt Sgt; Hampshire Regt Sgt; Somerset Light Infantry Sgt; Fusilier Regt Northumberland/Royal Munster/Royal Inniskilling Cpl and Sgt; School of Musketry Sgt; -?-; 2nd Lieut Territorial -?-; Devonshire Regt Sgt; Duke of Cornwall's Light Infantry L/Cpl.

THE YMCA WERE VERY ACTIVE IN THE TOWN during the years of the First World War and their work was particularly appreciated by the thousands of troops moving through the area on their way to and from the front. Some years later the movement purchased Belle Vue on the seafront (see p. 88 top). This happy bunch could have been photographed at one of several sites in the town, much of which was still occupied by canvas in 1919.

THE SALVATION ARMY HELD A NUMBER OF SUMMER CAMPS around the country in the early 1900s for both girls and boys. In 1907 a boys only camp was held at Herne Bay from 20 July to 17 August. The cost to the boys was 8s 6d (42½p) per week if aged under seventeen. The exact location of this picture is unknown although the site was almost certainly to the east of the town. One boy described the camp as some two and half miles from the railway station and a quarter of a mile from the sea. There were apparently good views of the country in almost every direction and a barn was available for use in inclement weather. Bathing was naturally a major feature of the holiday. The usual timetable of the day was as follows: rise at 7.00 a.m. and if fine bathe, breakfast at 8.00 a.m. followed by excursions, bathing or other amusements, dinner at 12.30 p.m., tea at 4.30–5.00 p.m., supper and evening prayers at 8.30 p.m., lights out at 9.30 p.m. On one day the officer in charge Major Trounce took a large party to Margate on a pleasure steamer. Musical evenings were arranged and attended by villagers (presumably from Beltinge). The vicar of Hoath visited the camp and Dr Vivian of the White House Hydro volunteered to act as medical advisor. His offer was gratefully received but his services were not needed.

VOLUNTARY AID DETACHMENT CAMP HERNE 1914. The VAD scheme was launched in 1909 when the British Red Cross Service and Order of St John combined to form voluntary aid detachments to supplement the activities of the Territorial Medical Service in war time. Camps were seen as the ideal way of testing members' training in first aid and nursing and the first county camp was held at Broomfield in 1913. In 1914 the official county camp was at Rolvenden; however in June of that year the Herne camp was repeated although on a different site from that used in 1913. Contemporary reports show that these camps were well organized on military lines. Camp standing orders ran to sixteen items: reveille was at 6.30 a.m. with lights out at 10.15 p.m. The day was filled with parades, drills, displays, lectures and tests. Detachments from the six divisions of Kent had to make their own way to camp, most arriving at Herne Bay by rail. The photograph of 'arrivals' shows the horse-drawn station omnibus being unloaded, and members were encouraged to bring their own bicycles. The large trunks on the roof might indicate a certain lack of camping experience from some members.

Stretcher party off to Canterbury
26
CAMP. Herne. 1914

There were rotas drawn up for all duties including the kitchens (this duty was excused parades). A Red Cross journal described as 'splendid experience' the opportunity for those who had never before done any housework, but who were called upon to scrape potatoes and wash saucepans. The photograph of members outside a tent provides a comparison between the uniforms of the two organizations. The Red Cross uniform on the right complete with blue felt hat, braid band and badge cost 3s 6d (17½p). On the first Sunday at the camp a private of the 6th Dragoon Guards fell from his machine while cycling past the camp field (the cause of his distraction is not recorded) and his injuries were attended to in the camp. Later in the week the band of the regiment was sent to the camp to provide entertainment in recognition of their kindly treatment.

Fire Drill

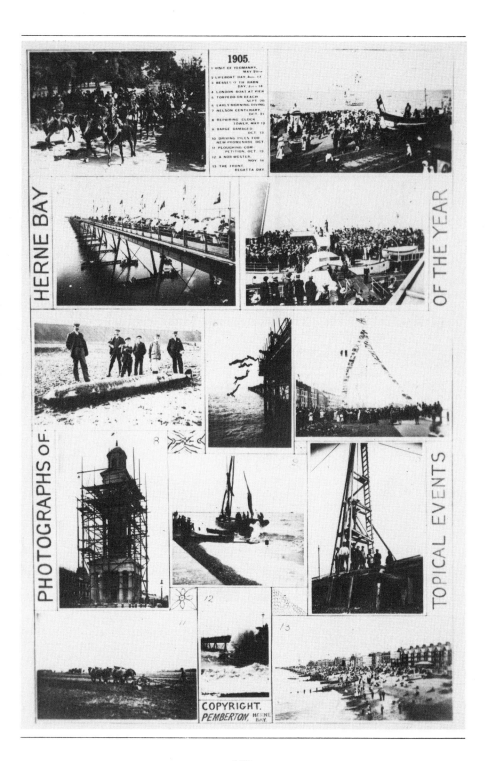

DURING THE SECOND WORLD WAR the pier pavilion was taken over for war work. These ladies produced camouflage nets stretched over wooden racks on the rink where a few years earlier thousands of people had applauded international skaters and entertainers. The particular relevance of the picture in this collection is that my mother is among the crowd of faces. Some of the names remembered are: Bomber, Collins, Pressley, Mount, Redman, Mills, Holness, Edwards, Frost, Marks, Bailey, Covell, Burton, Mills, Guy, Sands. Others are known only by their first names.

Opposite:

THIS MULTIVIEW POSTCARD combines a number of photographs. All taken by Pemberton through 1905, some appear elsewhere in this book. There is a tragic story connected with picture No. 8. In May the local builder Ingleton had his men erecting scaffolding on the Clock Tower. When the men stopped work to have their breakfast on Saturday 13 May a labourer Edward Henry Griggs took shelter inside the base of the tower. For some unknown reason a rope snapped and the heaviest of the clock weights (some 5 cwt) crashed through two floors and crushed Griggs. The man was rushed to hospital by the Ambulance Corps but despite amputating both legs Dr T.A. Bowes was unable to save the man.

ACKNOWLEDGEMENTS

The following organizations and individuals have freely given their time and expertise to assist me in compiling captions. Many happy hours have been spent exploring the memories triggered by these pictures. Available space dictates that many of the captions represent only the tip of an iceberg of reminiscence. I apologize to anybody that I have inadvertently omitted.

Royal Air Force Museum Hendon • National Motor Museum Beaulieu National Dairy Museum • Boulton & Paul plc • Royal Navy Submarine Museum • National Maritime Museum • The *Daily Mail* • Shepherd Neame Ltd • British Red Cross • The Scout Association • The Salvation Army Mr R. Morris of the Standard Motor Club • Whitbread Breweries Archive Department • All the staff at Herne Bay Library • Herne Bay Records Society Archive • Mr T.M. Littlewood • Herne Bay County Primary School • Noreen Chambers and Marshall Vine of the Medway Queen Preservation Society Canterbury and East Kent Postcard Club for the use of their Library • Bill Johnson • Mr and Mrs C.J. Barton • Harry Chalk • Jack Conrath • Sid Croft Mr W.G. 'Nobby' Clark • Mrs E. Davey • Alan Dilnot • Jack Edwards Ernie Holness • Peter Hoare • Mr Goodwin • Mr and Mrs R. Root • Jack and David Ridout • Mrs C.M. Mount • Harold Welch • Peter Walters • Mrs M.E. Pitt John Welch • Mr and Mrs P. Smoothy • Mrs F.A. Wacher • Roger Turner Mrs J. Douglas • Mr and Mrs H. Gough • Mrs S.A. Pateman • Roger Pout David Bubier • Eric Baldock.

My thanks also go to Pauline Marks for reading captions and the many collectors and dealers who have found photographs for me over the years. Finally my thanks go to my wife Tina who has typed manuscripts and who, along with my sons Ben, Tom and Sam, has provided patient encouragement through the past few months.